KATHERINE ANNE PORTER

In the same series:

MODERN LITERATURE MONOGRAPHS
GENERAL EDITOR: Lina Mainiero

KATHERINE ANNE PORTER

John Edward Hardy

Frederick Ungar Publishing Co.
New York

1973

Second Printing, 1976

To Willene

"I prey to God that it may plesen yow;
Thanne woot I wel that it is good ynow."

The texts of Miss Porter's fiction I have used are: *The Collected Stories of Katherine Anne Porter* (New York: Harcourt, Brace and World, Inc., 1965), and *Ship of Fools* (Boston and Toronto: Little, Brown and Co., 1962).

—J. E. H.

Contents

Chronology

* 1890:   15 May: Katherine Anne Porter born in Indian
              Creek, Texas, to Harrison and Mary Alice
              Jones Porter.

* 1892:   After death of Mary Alice, family moves to
              Kyle, Texas, to live with Harrison's mother,
              Catherine Anne Porter.

  1901–17:   Catherine Anne dies, and the family farm is
              sold shortly thereafter. In 1903 or 1904, Harri-
              son moves with his family to San Antonio.
              * Katherine Anne attends various private schools.
              . At the age of sixteen, she runs away from
              school and marries; at nineteen, she is divorced.
              . In 1911, she goes to Chicago, where she is em-
              ployed by a newspaper and by a film company
              as a bit player. In 1914, she returns to Texas
              and works for a time there and in Louisiana as
              a traveling entertainer, singing Scottish ballads. *
              . In 1917, she is on the staff of *The Critic*, a Fort
              Worth weekly newspaper.

  1918–19:   . Works as a reporter for *The Rocky Mountain
              News* in Denver, where she is critically ill with
              influenza. After her recovery, she moves to

New York, supporting herself by miscellaneous writing-for-hire.

1920:   Studies art in Mexico and witnesses events of the Obregón revolution.

1921–29: Returns to Fort Worth. Writes articles about Mexico. Acts in the Fort Worth Little Theater; writes "María Concepción" (1922). Travels again in Mexico, gathering materials for an exhibit of folk art. Returns to New York City, where she works on a biography of Cotton Mather and writes book reviews for various periodicals.

1930:   Publishes *Flowering Judas, and Other Stories.*

1931:   Lives in Mexico on a Guggenheim Fellowship. Departs for Europe in August, aboard a German ship, keeping a journal of the voyage that was to provide the basic materials for *Ship of Fools.*

1932:   Travels in Europe.

1933:   Marries Eugene Pressly, of the U.S. Foreign Service. Publishes a book of French songs, with translations.

1934:   Publishes "Hacienda."

1935:   Publishes expanded edition of *Flowering Judas, and Other Stories.*

1937:   Receives Book-of-the-Month Club award for *Noon Wine.* Divorces Eugene Pressly.

1938:   Marries Albert Erskine, Jr., of the Louisiana State University faculty. Receives second Guggenheim Fellowship.

1939:   Publishes *Pale Horse, Pale Rider.*

1940:   Receives first annual gold medal for literature, from Society of Libraries of New York University, for *Pale Horse, Pale Rider.* Modern Library edition of *Flowering Judas* collection is published.

1942: Publishes translation, with introduction, of José Joaquín Fernández de Lizárdi's *The Itching Parrot*. Divorces Albert Erskine. •

1943: Is elected a member of the National Institute of Arts and Letters.

1944: Publishes *The Leaning Tower, and Other Stories*.

1949: Accepts appointment as writer-in-residence and guest lecturer at Leland Stanford University. (Holds similar positions in later years at many other colleges and universities—including University of Chicago, University of Michigan, University of Liège, University of Virginia, Washington and Lee University.) Modern Library edition of *Pale Horse, Pale Rider* collection is published.

1952: • Publishes *The Days Before*.

1959: Receives Ford Foundation grant in literature.

1962: Receives O. Henry Memorial award for "Holiday." Publishes *Ship of Fools*, a Book-of-the-Month Club selection and best-seller. Receives Emerson-Thoreau Bronze medal of American Academy of Arts and Sciences.

1965: Publishes *The Collected Stories of Katherine Anne Porter*.

1966: Receives Pulitzer Prize and National Book Award for fiction.

1967: Publishes *A Christmas Story*.

1970: Publishes *The Collected Essays and Occasional Writings of Katherine Anne Porter*.

1972: Lives in College Park, Maryland.

1

Katherine Anne Porter: A Biographical Essay

Much of Katherine Anne Porter's fiction has the ring of autobiography. Even in stories with protagonists who are in no way identifiable with Miss Porter herself, persons and actions seem more the product of memory than of invention. In her Paris journal of 1936, she wrote that the "constant exercise of memory" was the "chief occupation" of her creative mind. "I must know a story 'by heart' and I must write from memory."[1]

But it is remarkable how few firmly established facts about her life are available. George Hendrick, in the opening chapter of his *Katherine Anne Porter*, remarks that Miss Porter herself "has been extremely reticent in revealing biographical information, especially about her early years."[2] And nothing of importance has been added to the public record since Hendrick's book was published in 1965. For the "facts" presented in the following sketch, I have relied chiefly upon entries in such standard biographical dictionaries as *Who's Who in America*, *Contemporary Authors*, and *Current Biography*; upon published interviews with Miss Porter by Barbara Thompson in *Paris Review*,[3] Archer Winsten in the New York *Post*,[4] and Robert van Gelder in *Writers and Writing*[5]; upon Glenway Wescott's "Katherine Anne Porter Personally," in *Images of Truth*[6]; and upon Hendrick's account in *Katherine Anne Porter*.

Katherine Anne Porter, third of the five children of Harrison and Mary Alice Jones Porter, was born in Indian Creek, Texas. The 1972–73 edition of *Who's Who in America* lists the date of her birth as 15 May 1890. After the mother's death in 1892 the family moved to Kyle, Texas, where the children were cared for by their paternal grandmother, Catherine Anne Porter. A Kentuckian who had moved to Texas sometime shortly after the Civil War, she owned both a house in Kyle and a farm nearby, at which she and her son and grandchildren frequently stayed. The stories of *The Old Order* provide the principal fictional account of the family's life during these years.

Mrs. Porter senior died in 1901. Sometime thereafter, both the house in Kyle and the farm were sold, and Harrison Porter and his family, in 1903 or 1904, settled in San Antonio.

The history of Katherine Anne Porter's education is obscure. Among "some facts," Glenway Wescott mentions in "Katherine Anne Porter Personally" that she "went to a convent school, perhaps more than one," and that "she spent an important part of her girlhood in New Orleans."[7] Perhaps her years in New Orleans were spent at such a school as that described in "Old Mortality."

It seems that she was precocious and rebellious both as a child and as a teen-ager—composing stories as soon as she had learned to write, directing and acting in plays at home, studying dramatics at school, and reading widely on her own. In an interview published in the *Paris Review* in 1963, she listed some of the reading she did in her youth: Shakespeare's sonnets, which brought her to a "turning point" in her life at the age of thirteen; translations of Dante and Homer, of Ronsard and other older French poets; Montaigne; and, at her father's suggestion, Voltaire's philosophical dictionary, in an edition with notes by Smollett; the eighteenth-century novelists; Emily Brontë, Dickens, Thackeray, Henry James, Thomas Hardy.[8] It is not really surprising that at the age of sixteen she ran away from school—according to the *Paris Review* interview "from New Orleans"[9]—and got married. Neither the critical studies nor the standard biographical dictionaries provide the name of her first husband. The marriage ended in three years.

Soon thereafter she moved to Chicago, apparently having found that there was no comfortable place in conservative Texas society for a young divorcee, especially for one who had the unladylike ambition of becoming a professional writer. For a while she was a reporter on a Chicago newspaper. She even worked several months as an extra with a movie company. Desperately poor, but determined to be independent, she stayed on in Chicago until 1914, when she passed up an opportunity to move to Hollywood with the film company. She then returned to Texas.

In the *Paris Review* interview of 1963, she spoke of having been a traveling entertainer at that time, singing Scottish ballads, in a costume she made for herself, "all around Texas and Louisiana."[10] In 1917, she was hired by a Fort Worth weekly, *The Critic*, as a writer of drama criticism and society gossip. The next year she moved to Denver, where she became a reporter for *The Rocky Mountain News*.

It would seem, from the reports of Wescott and others, that illness played an important part in the development of Miss Porter's character as artist. Her medical history, too, is obscure. According to Wescott, "when she was a girl somewhere in the South, she had to spend months and months in a sanitarium with a grave pulmonary illness, diagnosed as one of the baffling, uncommon forms of tuberculosis."[11] In the *Paris Review* interview, Miss Porter spoke of a similar episode just after her tour of Texas and Louisiana as a ballad singer: "And then I was supposed to have TB, and spent about six weeks in a sanitarium. It was just bronchitis, but I was in Denver, so I got a newspaper job."[12] It is not clear whether

Wescott and the interviewer for the *Paris Review*,
Barbara Thompson, have reported two inconsistent
accounts by Miss Porter of the same incident. The
much earlier report by Archer Winsten in the New
York *Post*, 6 May 1937, indicates that she contracted
tuberculosis in Chicago before her return to Texas in
1914.[13] Perhaps she was hospitalized several times, as
a girl and as a young woman, and in different places,
with tuberculosis or something mistaken for it. But,
whatever other illnesses she did or did not have while
she was in Denver, it seems certain that she almost
died there of influenza during the epidemic of 1918.
That experience, fictionalized in "Pale Horse, Pale
Rider," she spoke of many years later, in the *Paris
Review* interview, as the source of a quasi-mystical
insight into the realities of life and death and her own
selfhood that fundamentally and permanently altered
her moral outlook. "I really had participated in
death," she said to Barbara Thompson. "I knew what
death was, and had almost experienced it. I had what
the Christians call the 'beatific vision,' and the Greeks
called the 'happy day,' the happy vision just before
death. Now if you have had that, and survived it, . . .
you are no longer like other people, and there's no
use deceiving yourself that you are."[14]

Sometime late in 1919, apparently fully recovered
from her illness, she moved to New York City, where
she briefly earned a living as a hack and ghostwriter.
With the war over, she went to Mexico in 1920, as
an art student and as an enthusiastic and admiring witness of the Obregón revolution. As she explained in
"Why I Write about Mexico" (1923) the country
was already familiar to her, from her childhood
experience in San Antonio, where the influence of
Mexican culture is strong, and from the stories of her

father, who, she said, had "lived part of his youth in Mexico."[15] She speaks of having been in Mexico during the earlier Madero revolution, and of having witnessed then, "from the window of a cathedral," a street battle between the revolutionists and the government troops.[16] The visit to Mexico in 1920, however, was the beginning of her active interest in the country and its people.

By 1921, she was back in Texas, writing for a trade magazine, acting in the Fort Worth amateur theater. But for at least the next ten years of her unsettled existence, Mexico was the principal center of her intellectual life. She wrote articles on Mexican culture and politics for *Century Magazine*, and traveled again in Mexico gathering material on folk art. She went back to New York City in the 1920s, and wrote various reviews for such publications as the *Herald Tribune*, *The Nation*, and the *New Republic*. During this period she was also at work on a biography of Cotton Mather, a project certainly remote from her Mexican interests. But "María Concepción," based on her experience in Mexico and written in 1922, was the first of her published stories that she chose to preserve in collected editions. Another Mexican story, "Flowering Judas," was the title story of her first collection, published in 1930. When she was awarded a Guggenheim fellowship in the following year, she returned to Mexico.

This trip was made unhappy by an ugly and painful experience with Hart Crane, who, also in Mexico on a Guggenheim, rented a house next door to Miss Porter. The two had been very close friends. But Crane, already plainly suicidal and repeatedly involved in dangerous escapades of public drunkenness

and homosexuality, was a troublesome neighbor.
Apparently Miss Porter and other friends were often
called upon to rescue him. They were then expected
to listen to his maudlin, abusive monologues as a
reward for their pains. When Miss Porter failed to
show up for a dinner party to which he had invited
her, he went into town to get drunk and later ac-
costed her at her gate with obscene and frightening
curses. In a letter written long afterward, Miss Porter
vividly recalled how "he broke into the monotonous
obsessed dull obscenity which was the only language
he knew after reaching a certain point of drunkenness
[and] cursed things and elements as well as human
beings . . . the moon and its light . . . the air we
breathed together."[17]

Crane tried to discount the importance of the
incident, and to make amends; but, according to him,
she never accepted his apology. No doubt justly, he
rejected the charges by some of Miss Porter's friends
that, as he said, his "presence in the neighborhood was
responsible for a break or discontinuance of Katherine
Anne's creative work."[18] There is no evidence that
she ever allowed *anyone* to distract her very long
from her work when she truly wanted to stay at it.
But she had been genuinely fond of Crane. She
sincerely admired him as an artist. And it seems likely
that the death of their friendship contributed a great
deal to the mood of profound disillusionment that op-
pressed her when she went to Europe in 1931.

Miss Porter's voyage from Veracruz to Bremerhaven, aboard a German ship, provided the basic
materials for the long novel, *Ship of Fools*, that
appeared thirty years later. An interesting note on the
continuity of Miss Porter's imaginative experience is

George Hendrick's discovery that in her final, fictive
account of the voyage, incidents aboard the *Vera* recall her encounters with Hart Crane in Mexico.[19]

She stayed some time in Berlin, where, according
to her later statement, she met Hitler, Göring, and
Goebbels, all of whom she saw as "detestable and
dangerous." The Berlin experience yielded materials
for the short novel *The Leaning Tower*, as well as
for *Ship of Fools*. In 1933 she married Eugene
Pressly, a member of the American Foreign Service.
She lived several years in Paris, compiling a French
song book and writing fiction. In 1934 "Hacienda"
was published, and in 1935 an enlarged edition of the
Flowering Judas collection. When *Noon Wine* was
granted the Book-of-the-Month Club award in 1937,
she achieved her first considerable popular success.

Divorced from Pressly, she married Albert
Erskine, Jr., of the Louisiana State University faculty,
in 1938, and lived for several years in Baton Rouge.
In 1939, the *Pale Horse, Pale Rider* volume was
published. In 1942 her translation of José Joaquín
Fernández de Lizárdi's *The Itching Parrot* appeared.

She divorced Albert Erskine in 1942. In 1943,
she was elected a member of the National Institute of
Arts and Letters. *The Leaning Tower, and Other
Stories* appeared in 1944. Her position on the Leland
Stanford University faculty as writer-in-residence, to
which she was appointed in 1949, was the first of
several such posts she held during the next twelve
years. A collection of her critical and personal essays,
The Days Before, was published in 1952. "Holiday,"
published in 1960, received the O. Henry Memorial
award in 1962.

During the late 1950s, she returned to sustained
work on the long-delayed novel, earlier provisional

titles for which were "No Safe Harbor" and "Promised Land," and finished it in the spring of 1961. Fragments had appeared in various magazines; but some of Miss Porter's most faithful admirers, after so long a time, had ceased to believe she would ever complete it. Published in 1962 as *Ship of Fools*—a title taken from that of the late fifteenth-century allegorical satire *Das Narrenschiff*, by Sebastian Brant—it was an immediate best-seller.

A collected volume of her previously published stories and short novels appeared in 1965. Although she has published no new fiction since *Ship of Fools*, she received both the Pulitzer Prize and the National Book Award for fiction in 1966. *The Collected Essays and Occasional Writings of Katherine Anne Porter* was published in 1970. A biographical study of Cotton Mather, on which she first began work in 1928 and sections of which have appeared in print, is presumably still in progress. She lives now in College Park, Maryland.

In essays and interviews, and in sketches for such publications as *Who's Who in America*, Miss Porter herself has provided most of the information about her life that her critics have used. Many of the facts she records have not been independently verified. And her own statements are frequently inconsistent.

Her remarks about her art, as well as the stories themselves, often seem to invite biographical attention. She has repeatedly emphasized her reliance upon memory for story material. To be sure, she insists upon the artist's right, and duty, to reshape the materials provided by memory. "Yet in this endless remembering which surely must be the main occupation of the writer, events are changed, reshaped, interpreted again and again in different ways, . . .

because it is the intention of the writer to write fiction, after all—real fiction, not a *roman à clef*, or a thinly disguised personal confession which better belongs to the psychoanalyst's séance."[20] And the background experience includes "legend" and "acquired knowledge"—i.e., knowledge acquired from reading —as well as personal experience.[21] She also said: "My safety ground as a writer is based on what I saw or heard or experienced, a reality which I never get mixed up with fiction, only elaborate on."[22] It would be an interesting critical exercise to compare the fictional treatment of her experience to the facts of that experience if we could only be sure what the real-life facts are.

But on many points the record is obscure. According to George Hendrick:

Even her childhood religion is in doubt—her fictional family in the Miranda stories is Catholic, and her biographical sketches speak of her education in Catholic schools—but Texans who knew her as a child insist that the Porters were Methodists. Ray B. West, in early studies of Miss Porter and in his recent [1963] pamphlet *Katherine Anne Porter*, accepted the fictional Catholicism as fact and interpreted many of her stories in terms of the moral values of Catholicism; this interpretation was not challenged until recently, when Miss Porter asked Professor West to enter a correction about her religion in the University of Minnesota pamphlet.[23]

Professor Hendrick's next sentence—"Just when Miss Porter was converted is not now known; one of my informants thinks it was after her bout with influenza in Denver in 1918"[24]—only raises further questions. And it is "confusion worse confounded" to consider the circumstances, then, of how Miss Porter *lost* the Catholic faith she had come so dubiously by.

Explaining to Archer Winsten, in 1937, why she 7
had resisted the temptation to embrace Marxism, she ·
said: "Why should I have rebelled against my early
training in Jesuit Catholicism only to take another
yoke now?"[25] Why, indeed. But . . . "*Jesuit* Catholicism?" Who were these Jesuits? Just how early, and
where, and by what subtle means, did they collar her?
And how and when did she escape the bondage?

The case history of Miss Porter's "Catholicism" is
as obscure as that of her tuberculosis. And there is an
enviable, somehow even admirable, simplicity of purpose in M. M. Liberman's recent reassertion of what
might be called the original "West hypothesis." Liberman has surely read Hendrick's book, which was
published in 1965. But in *Katherine Anne Porter's
Fiction*, 1971, Liberman refers to Miss Porter's Roman
Catholic upbringing as if it were a matter of undis-
puted fact. Without presenting any new supporting
evidence, he blandly remarks that "Miranda's family
. . . are, as were Miss Porter's, Catholics."[26]

For a long time, in biographical sketches for
which she presumably supplied the information, the
year of Miss Porter's birth was listed as 1894—although her mother is supposed to have died in
1892.[27] Current articles indicate that she was born in
1890. But as recently as December 1971, in an essay
of personal reminiscence in *McCall's* magazine, she
has recorded memories of her childhood that again
raise questions about her age and about the date of
her mother's death. She recalls Christmas at home in
Texas, when after the long, tiring day of church-
going, present-opening, feasting, and quarreling, she
and the other children were put to bed by a company
of adults that included her mother. A precocious
two-year-old Katherine Anne must indeed have been

to have appreciated so fully as she did at the time the rarity of her privilege in being permitted to taste the holiday wines.[28]

As she presented it in the personal essay "Portrait: Old South," dated 1944, Katherine Anne's own family history is strikingly similar to Miranda's.[29] The portrait of Miss Porter's grandmother in this essay is much more sentimental than the characterization of Sophia Jane in the stories of *The Old Order*. But, though Miss Porter may adhere to her statement that she never gets reality "mixed up with fiction," she has not chosen to assist her public in avoiding such confusion. Who is to say that the portrait of the grandmother in the essay is any closer than the portrait of Sophia Jane in the stories to the "reality" of the woman who was the model for them both, or that either rendering better expresses Katherine Anne Porter's "real" feelings about her father's mother?

For anyone interested in the psychology of the artist, Katherine Anne Porter's evasiveness about her personal history may be a more rewarding subject of study than any number of particular, verified facts. And for those who simply want to read stories, and make some sense of them, Miss Porter's statement that what she tried to write was "real fiction" should be sufficient.

2

That Hideous Institution

When Cousin Eva, the spinster suffragette in "Old Mortality," bitterly condemns the family as a "hideous institution," one that is "the root of all human wrongs" and that ought to be "wiped from the face of the earth," she is somewhat consciously oversimplifying, and overstating, her own attitude. Certainly Eva's remarks alone do not adequately convey Katherine Anne Porter's complex views on the subject.

In her stories, the family is always supported in its evil work by other institutions—social, political, and religious. And in her treatment of evil in the family, just as in her treatment of corruption in politics and religion, she always holds an implicit vision of an ideal that has been vitiated, betrayed, or perverted.

But Miss Porter shares with Eva an almost obsessive preoccupation with family life, and with the struggle of the individual to maintain a personal identity—either within the family or, if need be, in anguished rebellion against it. The theme appears, more or less prominently, in almost every one of her stories, early and late. The consistency of her concern with it overrides all ethnic, regional, religious, and economic distinctions. Mexicans; Texans, white and black; German and Irish immigrants; farmers in Texas and Connecticut; Southern and Middlewestern schoolteachers and artists and journalists living in Mexico, Denver, New York, and Berlin; Protestants and Catholics and atheists—all, for good or ill, carry with them throughout their lives the burden of family consciousness.

For the most part, it is for ill rather than good. As Katherine Anne Porter represents it in her fiction, the lot of man is generally unhappy; her characters' moments of joy are extremely rare—although it ought to be added that the joy is totally convincing when it does occur, and the more to be appreciated for the very fact of its rarity. And, if the family itself is not the root of quite *all* the human wrongs she writes about, still it is seldom that anyone in her stories is helped by his family to cope with the evils that have their source elsewhere in nature and society. The family situation, either present or remembered, is at least a secondary source of the protagonist's unhappiness in almost all the stories. In almost half of them the "hideous institution" is the very fountainhead of misery.

This is the situation in "Old Mortality" and the stories of Miranda's family in the sequence of *The Old Order*[1]; in "Holiday," the long story of an anonymous narrator's vacation on the farm of a German immigrant family in Texas, where she befriends an afflicted daughter who functions as a menial servant; in "The Downward Path to Wisdom," which is about an unwanted child whose emotionally retarded parents and relatives use him as a weapon in their neurotic conflicts; above all in "He." Even in the two stories that are unusual for their expression of triumphant joy, "The Fig Tree" and "The Grave," Miranda's happy affection for some members of her family is bought at the expense of her alienation from others.

Throughout the stories of *The Old Order*—about Katherine Anne Porter's chief fictional counterpart, Miranda, and her family—images of death abound. Both Miranda's grandmother, Sophia Jane, and black Aunt Nannie, Sophia Jane's servant and companion who was once her slave, are all but constantly preoccupied with the dead; the past, the realm of the dead, is more real for them than the present.

"Even the future seemed like something gone and done with when they spoke of it. It did not seem an extension of their past, but a repetition of it." Sophia Jane preserves in elaborate trappings the mementoes of her forebears. She decorates her great-grand-mother's rolling pin with a covering of "an extra-ordinarily complicated bit of patchwork," and gold tassels on the handles. For the daguerrotype portrait of that "notably heroic captain of the War of 1812," her father, she contrives something suggestive of a portable reliquary, "a sort of envelope of cut velvet and violet satin, held together with briar stitching."

In the ceremonial burials they give to dead animals, with wooden tombstones carved by Uncle Jimbilly, Aunt Nannie's husband, the children imitate their elders' obsession. But the central theme of the final two stories in the series is the triumph of life over death.

The Fig Tree

The story opens with an account of the family's preparations for one of their annual summer visits to the country. As usual, old Nannie and the Grand-mother are figures of oppressive maternalism, curbing Miranda's eager high spirits.

Nannie, brushing the little girl's hair and fasten-ing a sunbonnet to her topknot with a safety pin, holds her firmly between her knees. "When Miranda wriggled, Aunt Nannie squeezed still harder, and Miranda wriggled more, but never enough to get away." As always, neither of the women will directly answer the child when she asks where they are going. She must figure it out from remarks exchanged among the adults. She and her father have a standing joke about the name of the farm, which he is reluctant to visit at this time of year because it is so hot. "The name of Grandmother's farm . . . was Cedar Grove, but Father always called it Halifax. 'Hot as Halifax,' he would say when he wanted to describe something very hot." In the father's phrase, Halifax, of course, is a euphemism for Hell. Obviously, no one has explained this to Miranda. But her Grandmother disapproves of her using the phrase. And when Miranda asks her whether they are going to Halifax, the old lady is typically prim and impatient, admonishing her to "call things by their right names," while at the same time refusing to simply say they are going to Cedar Grove.

Just before their departure, Miranda finds a dead baby chick in the yard and feels obliged to bury it with proper ceremony. She is quite sure that the chick really is dead; but when she has piled the dirt up over the grave, she is startled to hear a faint cry coming from somewhere. " 'Weep, weep,' said the tiny sad voice."

She puts her ear close to the ground, trying to locate the source of the cry. She cannot, and hearing the impatient clamor of the family's voices calling to her that they are ready to start, that she will be left behind if she does not hurry, she runs to get into the carriage. But the incident upsets her. Continuing to hear in her mind the tiny cry, she is in a frenzy of fear that she might have buried the chick alive.

They are joined at the farm by Sophia Jane's sister, Eliza. Great-Aunt Eliza is so unlike Grand-

mother that it is hard for the children to understand
how they can be sisters. Grandmother is slight, fine-
featured, and, despite her energy and will, feminine
and proper in every way. Eliza is big and homely;
she dresses in rough tweeds, climbs ladders like a man,
talks in a countrified, most unladylike way, and dips
snuff. She cultivates amateur scientific interests—
puttering around everywhere about the house with a
microscope, setting up a telescope on the roof of the
henhouse to look at the stars—which are most unusual
for a woman of her generation, and especially for
one of her provincial upbringing.

Sophia Jane tries to suppress her hostility to her
sister, but it breaks briefly into the open now and
again. She suggests to Eliza, who is climbing a ladder
onto the henhouse to set up her telescope, that she
should be more careful at her age. Eliza responds
tartly: "So long as you can go bouncing off on that
horse of yours, Sophia Jane, I s'pose I can climb
ladders. I'm three years younger than you, and *at your
time of life* that makes all the difference." Miranda is
obscurely disturbed by the spectacle of the two old
women quarreling like spiteful children; the solid and
dependable front of adult authority is being broken.

But, though she knows that her Grandmother
disapproves of her sister, she is irresistibly fascinated
by the gruff-voiced, kindly old mountain of a woman
who is Great-Aunt Eliza, with her earthy smell of
snuff and her coarse snuff-colored clothes. Miranda is
far too young to understand her own feelings, but
Eliza is a spirit of liberation for her, opening an un-
foreseen way of escape from the narrow, oppressive
moral and intellectual authority of the Grandmother.

In the most obviously symbolic episode, on the

evening of their arrival at the farm, Great-Aunt Eliza shows Miranda the moon through the telescope, and speaks to her of the "million other worlds" beyond the earth. But her imagination is only rather abstractly excited by this.

Miranda has her greatest joy in Great-Aunt Eliza's wisdom when she relieves her anxiety about the baby chick. Walking back to the house in the darkness, through the fig orchard, Miranda is suddenly frightened again by the sound she had almost forgotten during the afternoon. Having touched a branch of one of the trees, she hears all about her again, as if it were coming up from the ground, a chorus of the tiny, sad voices: "weep, weep." But Great-Aunt Eliza is able and willing to enlighten her. The cry does not come from the ground, she tells Miranda, but from the trees. It is the voice of the tree frogs, foretelling rain.

"Just think," said Great-Aunt Eliza, in her most scientific voice, "when tree frogs shed their skins, they pull them off over their heads like little shirts, and they eat them. Can you imagine? They have the prettiest little shapes you ever saw—I'll show you one some time under the microscope."

In the tree frogs' practice of eating their shed skins, there is a symbol of self-transcendence, of the victory of life over its own decay, that Miranda can comprehend no more fully than she could the "other world" of the moon that she saw through the telescope. But, for the moment, it is enough and more to know that the cry of "weep, weep," is the voice of the living, not the dead. The chick is dead, the frogs live. All in an instant, by the wonderful old woman's words, her heart is lifted up.

The Grave

Miranda is nine years old, and her brother Paul twelve. Grandmother has been dead for some years.

During the time of her widowhood, Sophia Jane had twice moved the body of her husband, first from Kentucky to Louisiana, and then to the farm in Texas. Over the years, his grave on the farm had become the nucleus of a small family cemetery. But after Grandmother's death, a part of her land, which includes the cemetery plot, is sold "for the benefit of certain of her children." The bodies are removed to the new public cemetery, where Grandmother herself is buried, and "at last her husband was to lie beside her for eternity, as she had planned."

One very hot summer day, Miranda and Paul are out with their rifles hunting for rabbits and doves, when they come to the fence that borders the old graveyard. They climb the fence and go exploring among the open pits where the coffins had been. In the grave that had been her Grandfather's, Miranda finds a tiny silver dove—"no larger than a hazel nut, with spread wings and a neat fan-shaped tail." In another grave, Paul discovers a ring. They compare treasures, and decide to exchange: Paul is fascinated by the dove, which he identifies as the ornamental head of a screw from a coffin, and Miranda is happy to have the "thin wide gold ring carved with intricate flowers and leaves," which she finds a perfect fit for her thumb.

Aware that they are trespassing, since the land no longer belongs to the family, they climb back over the fence to go on with their hunting for live game. Miranda is something of a tomboy, allowed by her father to dress in overalls for her romps in the fields and woods—"though it was making rather a scandal in the countryside, for the year was 1903, and in the back country the law of female decorum had teeth in it." But she is already beginning to entertain more mature, feminine visions of herself. She does not share her brother's serious enthusiasm for hunting, enjoying only the companionship and, as far as the guns are concerned, simply the excitement of pulling the trigger, whether she hits anything or not. On this day of the visit to the abandoned graveyard, she soon tires of following Paul about in the heat and thinks of going back to the house, to

take a good cold bath, dust herself with plenty of Maria's violet talcum powder—providing Maria was not present to object, of course—put on the thinnest, most becoming dress she owned, with a big sash, and sit in a wicker chair under the trees.

Only an impulse of guilty loyalty keeps her from turning back to let Paul go on alone—"Paul would never do that to her"—and leads her to the day's last adventure, that is to prove one of the most memorable and profoundly significant experiences of her life. Paul shoots a rabbit. Coming up beside him, she watches admiringly while he expertly skins the dead animal. Miranda reaches down to feel the exposed muscles, when Paul notices the "oddly bloated belly," and realizes that the rabbit was pregnant. " 'Look,' he said, in a low amazed voice. 'It was going to have young ones.' "

Removing the sac containing the baby rabbits from the rabbit's abdomen, he slits the sac itself so that they may see the tiny creatures plainly. Trembling, but not so much with disgust or fear as with awe, touched by the beauty of the little forms and by a nameless wonder at the mystery of life and death, Miranda looks with prolonged fascination. "She wanted most deeply to see and to know." And, "having seen, she felt at once as if she had known all along."

The knowing is a compact with her brother. She senses, although he does not tell her, that what they have seen is already familiar to him. And, no doubt rightly, afraid that their father will not approve of his "leading [her] into things" like this, Paul makes her promise not to tell anyone.

Paul puts the baby rabbits back into the body of the mother, to bury them together. And it would seem that the experience, too, is to be buried in Miranda's mind. She "never told, she did not even wish to tell anybody. She thought about the whole worrisome affair with confused unhappiness for a few days. Then it sank quietly into her mind and was heaped over by accumulated thousands of impressions. . . ."

But twenty years later, in a Mexican marketplace, "the episode of that far-off day leaped from its burial place before her mind's eye":

An Indian vendor had held up before her a tray of dyed sugar sweets, in the shapes of all kinds of small creatures: birds, baby chicks, baby rabbits, lambs, baby pigs. . . . It was a very hot day and the smell in the market, with its piles of raw flesh and wilting flowers, was like the mingled sweetness and corruption . . . that other day in the empty cemetery at home: the day she had remembered always until now vaguely as the time she and her brother had found treasure in the opened graves. Instantly upon this thought the dreadful vision faded, and she saw clearly her brother, whose childhood face she had forgotten, standing again in the blazing sunshine, again twelve years old, a pleased sober smile in his eyes, turning the silver dove over and over in his hands.

In its compact richness, its unforced handling of a complex symbolism not so much invented as chosen, its exquisite sensuous and psychological detail, "The Grave" is one of Miss Porter's finest stories. Its wealth of implicit meaning is inexhaustible.

But it becomes clear that the greatest treasure the day of the hunt yields for Miranda is not the man-made things she and Paul find in the abandoned graves. These things, the gold ring and the silver dove, they exchange but do not share. But they share the memory of the dead rabbit with her unborn young. (Miranda explicitly refuses to keep the rabbit's pelt, which ordinarily she would have taken to make a coat for a doll; she does not want any material souvenir of the occasion.) The ring, probably a wedding band, is associated with the dead past, something representative of the hold that her grandmother's essentially morbid spirit has upon her—that spirit of obsession with the dead that drove the widow to refuse to let her husband's bones lie in peace until they could be beside her own. The dove, which Paul is holding in the mind's-eye picture that comes to Miranda in the Mexican marketplace, is a traditional Christian symbol of the soul's immortality. But, of itself, it has little psychological power. The vitalizing image for Miranda is that of the baby rabbits, her long-buried memory of which is evoked by the sight of the candy animals on the vendor's tray. Emerging from the welter of her other sensations in the marketplace (which first woke a "dreadful vision" of the old graveyard on the farm), the recollection of the rabbits, and her

memory of the communion she had with her brother
at the sight of the little bodies he had delivered unborn
into death, produce at last a serene and triumphant
vision of life.

In its totality, and in the central image of the
rabbits, the young buried in the tomb of their
mother's body, the story acknowledges the mysterious
interdependence of life and death. But the final
thrust is toward life. The act of memory itself, the
fundamental act of human imagination, defeats the
power of time. But it is further significant that the
controlling image here is a *natural* one. In Words-
worth's phrase, Miranda's days are "bound each to
each by natural piety."

 Whatever of continuing good, for the present and
the future, Miranda derives from her experience on
Grandmother's farm, stems not from any "old order"
of a social and economic system, of hereditary prop-
erty rights, but from the earth itself on which that
order was built. The sacred center of her life, the
source of her sense of a vital and significant continuity
in her experience, is in the fields where she and her
brother knelt together in communion over the beauty
of the wild creatures.

The immediate source of the title for the series,
as William Nance pointed out, is Tennyson's *Morte
d'Arthur*: "The old order changeth, yielding place
to new." But the oldest order of all is unchanging.

Old Mortality

"Old Mortality" is the story of Miranda's growing up. It is divided into three dated sections. In the
first, 1885–1902, we are told of events in the lives of

the elders, which, as a "living memory," dominate the consciousness of Miranda and her older sister, Maria, during their childhood.

Miranda is eight years old at the end of this period, and Maria twelve. Motherless for many years, the little girls have been raised by their father, Harry, and their grandmother—with the assistance of various aunts, uncles, and older cousins. Both the father and the grandmother are dedicated to the preservation of an idealized picture of the family's past. The central legend is the "tragic" life of Harry's dead sister, Amy. Universally acknowledged as the greatest *belle* of her time, high-spirited and independent, she was bravely, almost joyfully undismayed by her conviction that she was destined for an early death. She established herself as the romantic heroine of the family when her second cousin, Gabriel, a patient and long-suffering suitor, felt himself obliged to challenge an offensive rival to a duel. To prevent the duel, her brother Harry created a disturbance by taking a pot-shot at the man. He then fled to Mexico to escape prosecution for attempted murder. Some time later, Amy finally accepted Gabriel's often-repeated proposal of marriage. But, faithful to her own prophecies, six weeks after the wedding she died.

Miranda's childish imagination is nourished on the endlessly repeated anecdotes of Amy's adventures. No one of the present generation of young ladies, however lovely and accomplished, can begin to rival Amy. No one does, or ever could, walk so well, ride so well, dance so well. No one can match the wit and verve, the sense of inexhaustible excitement, with which she lightly bore the burden of her tragic destiny.

Miranda, as well as her sister Maria who was

"born sensible," has some doubts even as a child
about the truth of the family myth. She questions,
for example, how it is that her father can say that
"there were never any fat women in the family, thank
God," in face of the existence of a certain enormous
aunt from Kentucky, whose husband will not allow
her to ride his horses for fear of their being injured.

But she does not begin to appreciate the truly
morbid character of her elders' preoccupation with
the past—especially of their apotheosis of the dead
Amy—until the episode that is the climax of Part
II, dated 1904. The sisters have been for some time
attending a convent school near New Orleans. On
one of his infrequent weekend visits, their father takes
them to the racetrack.

Uncle Gabriel's horse, Miss Lucy, is running.
And, with considerable misgiving, Miranda is persuaded in the name of family loyalty that the dollar
she has been given for betting should be risked on
Miss Lucy. Although a hundred-to-one long shot, the
horse wins. But the joy of the occasion is irreparably
damaged for Miranda by the shock of her first meeting with "romantic Uncle Gabriel." For so many
years the girls had listened with wonder and admiration to the story of his lifelong devotion to the
memory of Amy. In plain, present fact, Uncle Gabriel
is an aging drunkard, bleary-eyed, shambling, coarse-
talking. And when, after the race and the further
disheartening sight of the victorious Miss Lucy with
blood running from her nostrils, the sisters are taken
to Gabriel's shabby apartment on Elysian Fields, the
real human cruelty of the Amy myth is revealed.

Gabriel has repeatedly assured their father that
his present wife, Miss Honey, will be delighted to
receive them. But, as it turns out, Miss Honey has not

the slightest interest in them, indeed in anything that her husband brings home to her—including the news of Miss Lucy's victory. Having suffered for many years from Gabriel's ineptitude and his preoccupation with his first wife (the little girls are introduced to her with words about their resemblance to Amy), the resentful, embittered Miss Honey makes no effort to conceal her distaste for the visit. The sisters go back to the convent feeling rebuffed, and somehow cheated of their rightful pleasure in the holiday.

In the final part, dated 1912, Miranda is on her way to attend the funeral of Gabriel—who, of course, is to be buried at his request beside Amy. We learn that Miranda has run away from school, almost a year before, and married. On the train, she meets Cousin Eva, the ugly duckling of her father's generation. After the old lady recognizes Miranda, whom she knew as a child, and introduces herself, they fall into conversation. Cousin Eva, who is famous in the family for her homeliness, her classical learning, and her championship of the vote for women, entertains Miranda with certain reminiscences that, for the first time in her experience, explicitly challenge the romanticism of the family in general and specifically the legend of Amy. Eva asserts that Amy did have enemies, that she was not, as the myth would have it, universally admired, and even hints that her celebrated tragic destiny may have been effected by suicide.

Miranda—sympathetic to the old lady in her frank admission of the resentment she has felt all her life at her mother's overreadiness to assign her, even as a child, to the role of the "plain girl" in a beauty-oriented society—for a time finds Eva refreshing. Many of the things she says, in her open condemnation of the family's traditional romanticism, seem to lend support to Miranda's own efforts to define realistic values for herself.

But, in the end, when they reach their destination and are met by Miranda's father, Miranda feels once more cut off from all her elders. It is clear that her father has not fully forgiven her for her elopement. And, for all Eva's moral courage and intellectual independence, she and Harry still make common cause of their age, in unconscious opposition to the claim of youth. Seeing the essential warmth and affection with which her father and Eva greet each other, subtly excluding her from the circle of their understanding, Miranda resigns forever, as futile and pointless, the effort to comprehend the past. She silently asserts her determination henceforth to be concerned only with the truth about herself and her own experience.

The title of the story, as George Hendrick pointed out, ultimately derives from that of a novel by Sir Walter Scott.[3] Its internal source is the verse Gabriel wrote for Amy's gravestone:

> She lives again who suffered life,
> Then suffered death, and now set free
> A singing angel, she forgets
> The griefs of old mortality.

The little poem quite accurately defines the family's basic attitudes toward life and death. Gabriel has written more truly than we can suppose him to have consciously intended. Amy, with all the romanticist family, indeed regarded life, as much as death, as something to be "suffered." The state of "mortality" was one that offered only grief, one to be escaped as quickly as possible. The desire for escape is the basic motivation of the family's preoccupation

with the past and with the dead, a body of experience
that is safely beyond the threats of time, and that can
be manipulated at will, in imaginative remembrance,
to make it conform to the romantic ideal. Finding
her own vital impulses frustrated by the family pieties
Miranda more and more consciously tries to establish
for herself an attitude whereby she can accept the
state of mortal existence for what it is, not denying
the facts of its departure from any ideal. In the
courage of that very realism she hopes to find a
superior basis for optimism and joy.

But Miranda has not only the others to contend
with in her quest. Within her own soul runs a strong
strain of the family romanticism, the fatal capacity
and need to fictionalize experience. A significant example is her pleasure in thinking of herself and her
sister as "immured" in the convent where they go to
school. "Immured" is a word she has picked up from
a volume of anti-Catholic stories the girls found in an
attic during vacation at their grandmother's farm—
gothic tales of the horrors endured by "beautiful but
unlucky maidens . . . 'immured' in convents where
they were forced to take the veil . . . and condemned
forever after . . . to divide their time between lying
chained in dark cells and assisting other nuns to bury
throttled infants."

To imagine herself "immured" is infinitely pref-
erable, for Miranda, to admitting the rather dull facts
of their confined and routine-ridden, but not uncomfortable, existence at the convent. She indulges the
same tendencies of mind, exhibited in more and more
serious contexts, into young womanhood. And it is, of
course, in this *internal* struggle, the conflict of impulses within Miranda's own soul, that the central
dramatic tension of the story is generated.

As in all Miss Porter's fiction, the universals of
"Old Mortality" are immediately recognizable. It is a
story about growing up, about the conflict of youth
and age, and of realism and idealism, that could in its
philosophic essence belong to any place and era. But it
is a story rich in particulars, too, about the conflict
of a particular idealism with particular realities, about
a particular child growing up in a particular time and
place.

It is, for one thing, very much a southern story.
The romanticism of Miranda's elders is typical of the
agrarian upper-class, provincial mentality of the south
in the latter part of the nineteenth century. Sir Walter
Scott's chivalric novels exerted great influence upon
the imagination of that society.

The key word is "chivalry." The story might be
seen as a fictive examination of this concept and its
viability.

It is no accident that the central episode involves
a horse race. Chivalry is a complex body of social
and moral ideas. A central concept is the ideal of male
dedication to the protection and praise of womanhood. But, etymologically, *chivalry* is horsemanship;
the *chevalier* is the rider, the mounted man.

"Old Mortality" is not a blatantly feminist work.
Cousin Eva, the chinless suffragette, is finally a comic
character, more pathetic than admirable. But it is
important that the protagonist of the story is female.
Her search for identity, and for freedom, is to a great
extent identifiable with the struggle of modern southern woman to escape from the role to which the
chivalric tradition of the nineteenth century had assigned her—a role that Miss Porter clearly sees as one
of subjection. However subtly the men might have

disguised it as apotheosis of woman, and however willingly the women themselves might have acquiesced in the deception, the status of the female under the chivalric code was slightly lower than the fully human rather than higher.

Miranda, in the innocence of her childhood, dreams of becoming a jockey—in short, of becoming a man. But there is multiple irony in Great-Uncle John Jacob's comment on his refusal to allow his two-hundred-and-twenty-pound wife, Keziah, to ride his good horses: " . . . my sentiments of chivalry are not dead in my bosom; but neither is my common sense, to say nothing of charity to our faithful dumb friends. And the greatest of these is charity." John Jacob is closer to the truth of where women stand in the scale of values of the "chivalrous" male, when he frankly chooses to protect his horse's health at the expense of his wife's vanity.

The same theme is elaborated, in a more obviously serious vein, in the account of the race and the little girls' meeting with Gabriel and Miss Honey. The comic sense is still here, but it is a darker comedy now. Gabriel's devotion to horses, and to the elusive dream of permanently installing himself and Miss Honey in the splendor of a suite at the St. Charles Hotel on the proceeds of his gambling, is of a piece with his alcoholism as evidence of his moral irresponsibility and his refusal to see his second wife's bitter suffering. The horse he enters in this particular race is, moreover, a mare. And she shares with her owner's wife the euphemistic indignity of the appellation "Miss." The first time through the story, a reader may find it difficult to follow which, Miss Lucy or Miss Honey, is the horse and which the wife. The confusion is undoubtedly deliberate on Miss Porter's part. That old-fashioned Southern habit of calling a married woman Miss, as if she were eternally virgin, is an offshoot of the chivalric myth. The dubious nature of the compliment, which really amounts to denying the recipient her rights and dignity as a mature woman, to denying the virtue of sexual fulfillment, is underscored in this case by the association of horse and woman. Woman in a society whose values are so ordered, Katherine Anne Porter suggests, is not only not the rider but the ridden. Whether her name be Honey or Lucy, the exhausted and bleeding mount that bears drunken Gabriel as he plunges on in the mists of his absurd dream is emphatically feminine.

Finally, however, it is apparent that the men are equally the victims of the dream. The emphasis in the last section is on humanity, on the struggle between the young and the old, rather than between the sexes.

There is the implicit suggestion that the social and moral code of chivalry, and the system of blood loyalties that it involves—that "hideous institution" (the family) that Cousin Eva so bitterly denounces as "the root of all human wrongs"—may be evil only because it is historically obsolescent. It is as obsolescent as the horse itself, which, in the early years of the twentieth century, is beginning to lose its traditional functions except in the realm of sport. But it dies hard. Miranda is shrewd in seeing that Cousin Eva's analysis of the spiritual malady of her generation, her picture of Amy and the others as morbidly "sex-ridden," is "every bit as romantic" as all the rest she has been told about her elders. But if the vote for women and the "realism" of the new psychology of sex cannot provide the basis for new social institutions to accommodate the vital human impulses that the old forms threaten to stifle, then what can? It is for this way to truth that Miranda is desperately searching at the end of the story.

Miss Porter has no answer. This is a work of fiction, not a tract of any kind. It is clear only that the author's attitude at the end is not identical with that of her protagonist. During the ride home from the station, Miranda "hoped no one had taken her old room, she would like to sleep there once more, she would say good-by there where she had loved sleeping once, sleeping and waking and waiting to be grown, to begin to live."

We see here the pathetic falsity of all Miranda's brave "resolutions" to reject the myths of her family and seek the truth of her own existence without illusion. Like her thoughts about her marriage—"she knew now why she had run away to marriage, and she knew that she was going to run away from marriage" —her purpose to "know the truth about what happens to [her]" actually represents a reversion to childhood. It is a purpose undertaken under the greatest of all human illusions, that of the wish for a renewal of innocence.

Whatever the possibility of instituting new social forms that could contain the forces of "blood" that involve human beings with one another ("her blood rebelled against the ties of blood"), Miss Porter plainly rejects Miranda's dream of innocence, of starting over. The last word of the story is of crucial significance. It is only in her "ignorance"—which is a kind of *deliberate* ignorance, by no means synonymous with innocence—that Miranda can assure herself she "doesn't care" about her family and their myths, can hope to find some "truth about what happens to [her]," independently of any interest in the truth about others.

He

"He" is the idiot son of a poor farm family, the Whipples. The personal pronoun, capitalized throughout the story, is the only "name" the boy has. If the parents ever gave Him another name, they have ceased to use it.

Mrs. Whipple is fond of saying that she loves the idiot better than anyone else. But neither she nor Mr. Whipple pampers Him. Physically strong, and fearless, apparently able to take simple instructions although He cannot speak intelligibly, He does more than his share of the work on the farm. And He can be entrusted with some tasks, such as tending the bees and taking a suckling pig from the ferocious sow, that His older brother and sister are afraid to undertake. On one occasion, when His sister falls sick during a hard winter, Mrs. Whipple does not hesitate to take the blanket from His bed as extra cover for the girl, since He has always seemed insensitive to the cold.

But toward the end of the winter when He is ten years old, He becomes ill. On the doctor's orders, he must be given very special care if pneumonia is to be averted. He is to be fed well, with lots of milk and eggs. And, until the weather improves, the parents take a blanket off their own bed to put on His.

He seems to recover during the ensuing spring, summer, and fall. (Meanwhile, the other children have gone away, one to school, the other to a job in town.) But one day shortly before Christmas, coming up from the barn to the house, He slips and falls on the ice.

After the accident He is unable to stand on His

swollen legs. He is more than ever mindless and unresponsive. After a time, the doctor suggests that they take Him to the county home, where He can get proper daily care and will be "off [their] hands." Mrs. Whipple at first protests. She does not want charity. Nor does she want to have her neighbors say that she sent her sick child to live among strangers. But at length she is persuaded—by her husband's argument that his taxes as much as anyone's pay for the county services, so that it is not charity but their right. She accepts a neighbor's offer to drive her and Him to the home. The mother and son sit on the rear seat of the wagon.

On the way, she tries to convince herself that she is doing what is best for Him, as well as for herself and her husband and their normal children. But she is increasingly uneasy. And when He suddenly starts to weep, she is overwhelmed with sharp remorse. She thinks that He may be remembering the time she boxed his ears, the fear He must have felt the time they sent Him off alone to lead home a dangerous bull, the time they took His blanket for His sister and left Him to sleep cold.

Although continuing to argue with her conscience that she has done the best she knew how, that she could do little against a merciless fate, she fears that He has felt Himself overworked and abused. His accusations are the more terrible for the fact that He is unable to put them into words. She cries out in her soul that it would have been better if He had never been born. And the neighbor drives on, "not daring to look behind him."

The center of interest is in the relationship of the mother and child. The brother and sister, even the father, as well as the doctor and relatives and neighbors, are characters of only incidental importance, their actions significant only as they impinge upon the drama of Mrs. Whipple's obsession with Him.

Mrs. Whipple is pleased to call her obsession love. But the questionable accuracy of that term is the most obvious irony of the story. The other Whipple children are constantly hurting themselves and falling ill; He, it seems for many years, can do anything and never get a scratch. The preacher offers the pious explanation that "The innocent walk with God— that's why He don't get hurt." Mrs. Whipple often repeats the words, and they are a great comfort to the poor woman whenever she recalls them: " . . . she always felt a warm pool spread in her breast, and the tears would fill her eyes." But, for practical purposes, this idea that He enjoys God's special protection is valuable to the mother as an excuse for her own neglect and exploitation of Him.

Like other professed Christian pietists in Miss Porter's fiction, Mrs. Whipple is notably lacking in humility. Indeed, in all her most decisive actions she is principally motivated by pride: pride of possessions and of reputation.

Her pride in material wellbeing is one that has been severely tested in the luckless economy of the family. The motif of the "hardness" of their lot is established at the very beginning—"Life was very hard for the Whipples. It was hard to feed all the hungry mouths, it was hard to keep the children in flannels during the winter, short as it was. . . ." Mrs. Whipple yearns for prosperity. But sometimes her ambition is self-defeating. For example, over her husband's prudent protest, she roasts a suckling pig, sacrificing its future market value, to celebrate the visit of her brother and his family.

And, such is the eternal nature of pride, the more it is chastened, the stouter it grows. It seems to Mrs. Whipple that everything conspires to keep her and her family in unending poverty and anxiety. She sees Him as only the most severe of the many hindrances an unkind fate has thrown in the way of her rightful progress to the good life. But paradoxically, He provides perhaps her best opportunity to turn the tables on that fate.

His strength and presumably witless courage can be put to good practical use in the farm work. Since He cannot go to school anyway, and seems impervious to cold, the money that would otherwise have to be spent on His clothing and bedding can be spent on the other children. And she can hope to gain a good name among her neighbors for her display of cheerful devotion to the unfortunate child.

There are evidences of an intelligence and sensitivity in Him that might have been cultivated. Although retarded, He had begun to learn a few words before suffering a head injury in early childhood. And, on the occasion of the uncle's visit, He is plainly disturbed at the sight of the suckling pig slaughtered and dressed, and will not eat at the table with the family. But it is inconvenient for Mrs. Whipple to notice these things; so, she does not.

In the end, of course, her cruel folly is severely punished. Charity, the central Christian virtue, is offensive to Christian Mrs. Whipple's pride. Above all things, she fears being pitied by her neighbors. "Nobody's going to get a chance to look down on us," she says. And it is easy justice on the reader's part to refuse her what she so despises. There is something ugly and self-centered even in her final grief, in her interpretation of His sobs only as reproaches to her. She is herself so incapable of genuine charity, of love, that she cannot recognize even the possibility that His weeping is an expression of love for her—an appeal, simply, that He not be turned out of the family, rather than a reproach for what He has suffered there.

But there is the suggestion, too, that Mrs. Whipple's incapacity is the common incapacity of mankind, the curse of our intelligent being. Life is indeed "too hard" for most of us to be able to sustain such love as He, in His innocence, may feel. If, like the neighbor driving the wagon, we dare not look behind us, it is the essential, universal, and eternal misery of the human condition that we cannot countenance.[4]

3

Black and White

Black characters, all of them servants to white families, figure prominently in very few of Katherine Anne Porter's stories. Their personalities and behavior are of interest chiefly in the way that they reflect, and to some extent influence, the lives of the whites.

The portraits of the two ex-slaves, Nannie and her husband, Uncle Jimbilly, in "The Journey," "The Last Leaf," and "The Witness," and the characterization of the black girl, Dicey, who is little Miranda's reluctantly devoted nurse in "The Circus," are memorable both for their individuality and for their insight into the typical psychology of the Negro servant. Implicit in these stories is a trenchant criticism of Southern white paternalism, the conventional, hypocritical pretense of the masters that they regard the blacks as "real members of the family." The "hideous institution," even in comparatively enlight- functions at its subtle worst in assigning the blacks ened households like that of Miranda's family, to roles that deny them full human dignity. But, possibly just because she, like Miranda, was raised in a way that prevented her from knowing any Negroes during her formative years except on terms dictated by the system of social caste, Miss Porter never attempted a full-scale characterization of a black who is interesting primarily in his or her own right.

Old Nannie is the black shadow of Sophia Jane, who, only after her mistress is dead, in "The Last Leaf," pathetically asserts her right to independence by moving out of the "big house" to a cabin of her own on the place. Even in her refusal to let Uncle Jimbilly share the cabin, which is itself a sufficiently melancholy instance of human rejection, one cannot be sure that she is not simply following Sophia Jane's example of contempt for men. Uncle Jimbilly has

little to justify his existence except his carving of
wooden tombstones and his function as a "witness"—
of questionable reliability, mainly for the benefit of
the children—to the horrors of black slavery before
the Civil War. Dicey, of "The Circus," when she has
to leave the show to take care of the squawling
Miranda, who has been frightened by a clown and a
dwarf, demands a certain sympathy as the innocent,
incidental victim of the white child's hypersensitivity.
But it is not enough to distract the reader's primary
attention from Miranda's experience.

Only in "Magic," a very short story—signifi-
cantly, a story that does not belong to the autobiographical series—does Miss Porter distinctly identify
with the black woman. Here too, the black's consciousness is not directly explored; and she has to
evaluate her fortune in terms of the white households
in which she serves. But in the time present of the
story, she is in complete control of the situation. The
white woman to whom she is talking is interesting
only for her reactions to the words of the black.

Magic

In this exquisitely wrought satiric vignette, a
scant three pages long, the story is told all but entirely by implication. The frame situation involves a
New Orleans lady of quality, Madame Blanchard, and
her personal maid. The loquacious servant is dressing
her mistress's hair. She has overheard Madame's remark earlier, to the laundress, that she thinks someone
must have bewitched the sheets because so many of
them fall apart in the wash. Now she feels prompted
to tell an anecdote on the theme of witchery. Her

people, she explains, are the Louisiana Negroes of mixed French blood among whom the practice of sorcery is traditional.

The sordid story she tells is of an episode in the "fancy house" where she formerly worked as a chambermaid. The ruthless madam of the brothel had habitually cheated her whores. When she was accused of this by one Ninette, who announced her intention of leaving the house, the madam mercilessly beat the frail girl, with special attention to her private parts, and threw her out bleeding, penniless, and half-naked, into the street. After a few days, when men coming to the house repeatedly asked about the missing whore, the madam realized that she had made a business mistake in giving way to her rage. She enlisted the help of a Negro voodoo specialist among her servants in an effort to find Ninette and lure her back. A potion was made and due rituals performed. Sure enough, after seven nights the girl returned, still sick, but happy to be back. "And after that she lived there quietly."

It is sufficiently obvious that Ninette was not brought back to the bawdyhouse by the power of the magic spell. She came back, of course, simply because she had learned that there was nowhere else for her to go.

Similarly, Madame Blanchard's maid, whose relationship with her mistress is the center of the story, has another than her ostensible motive for telling the anecdote. How much she "believes in" magic remains questionable. But she certainly cannot actually intend, as she ironically suggests, that the dreadful tale will "rest" Madame Blanchard while her hair is brushed.

The story begins with the servant's saying, "And,

Madame Blanchard, believe that I am happy to be here. . . ." At the end, she remarks that the wretched Ninette, returning to the brothel and the cruel madam, was "happy to be there." The repetition of the phrase is significant for defining the servant's subtly malicious intent in telling the anecdote.

She is routinely flattering to her mistress and so-licitous of her comfort. She assures her that she is happy in her place in the "serene" household of the Blanchards. She begs her pardon when the lady pro-tests that her hair is being pulled in the brushing. And so on. But all the while she is slyly undercutting the flattery. She pretends to think, and obviously ex-pects Madame Blanchard to *know* she is only pretend-ing, that perhaps the grand lady does not even know what a fancy house is. She digresses briefly from her story to note that, although she is "colored," she has some of the same French blood in her that is the proud heritage of the Blanchards.

Madame Blanchard's superiority, defined in her name, is one of caste as well as color. But the maid, who has seen in the lady's sarcastic remark to the laundress a genteel version of the brothel madam's abuse of her whores, is determined that her mistress shall not be allowed to think that her "whiteness" is impervious to all stain of human misery and de-pravity.

Madame listens to the ugly story without appar-ent distress. After interrupting to protest at having her hair pulled, she even prompts the maid to go on with the narrative. She is either callous, or smug, or re-markably self-possessed. It is an essential part of the author's design that we not know which.

At what level of moral awareness *Madame* per-mits herself to ponder the validity of her superiority to the whores' *madam* we are not informed. And we are hardly to suppose that the maid is aware of all the fine ironies and the universal implications of her narrative. But hairdresser Porter tugs both hard and deftly enough that any reasonably sensitive "Blanchard" of a reader must be left wary of assuming the permanent safety of any escape from the bawdyhouse of the world.

4

*Man
and Woman*

Katherine Anne Porter's childless couples are, if anything, even more miserable than the mothers and fathers in her fiction. In the descriptions of their stifling lives together, all the vices of the "hideous institution" are painted in intense miniature.

Typically, one or the other is frigid, or impotent, or otherwise sexually deficient; sometimes, it is both. It is clear that some of these spouses sought in marriage a refuge from their families and only find themselves harnessed into a still more oppressive bondage to each other. One such couple is the poet-journalist and his first wife in "That Tree," who act out in Mexico a fantasy of escape from the effects of their puritan upbringing.

The middle-aged New York Irish couple of "A Day's Work" do have a married daughter, but she no longer lives with them. In most respects, the life of the Hallorans runs true to the type of the childless unions. The viciously puritanical wife has robbed her husband of his pride and his manhood. Her rigid pietism and propriety lead her to forbid him the kind of associations he would like to cultivate with men of the world. Thus her narrowness offers him an excuse for his natural laziness, and he is condemned to embittered failure. Old before his time, out of work, reduced to cadging drinks and money from petty politicians and daydreaming of a chance to join them in their shady enterprises, Halloran is a study of the uxorious man who is hopelessly bound to his wife by soured love and enmity.

In "Rope," a young city couple summering in the country fall into a bitter quarrel over the husband's selfish absent-mindedness. On a shopping trip into town, he forgets to buy the coffee that his wife repeatedly reminded him to get. But, indulging an absurd whim, he buys a large coil of heavy rope, for which he has no definable use, and tires himself carrying it on the walk home. The rope, of course, symbolizes the invisible bond of their destructive but probably unbreakable union. They are "at the end of the rope" of their patience with each other; they have "enough rope," with which to hang themselves. But they cannot work free of each other. At the end of the story, exhausted by a long exchange of recriminations, they are temporarily reconciled. But it is plain that they are doomed to resume the quarrel once they have rested. Referred to only as "he" and "she," they have all but lost their personalities in the degrading, continuous struggle that is their marriage.

But, despite a varied technical brilliance—the management of stream-of-consciousness techniques in "Rope" and "A Day's Work," the mastery of the Irish idiom in "A Day's Work," the manipulation of point of view in "That Tree," the complex use of symbolism in all of them—in none of these shorter stories on marriage is a character developed for whom full human sympathy is possible. Only one very long story on marriage is among Katherine Anne Porter's major achievements.

The Cracked Looking-Glass

Rosaleen O'Toole is the discontented wife of a man thirty years her senior. Both are Irish immigrants. When Rosaleen first met Dennis, he was head-waiter in a New York restaurant, and she a domestic servant. Now, they have lived for many years on a farm in Connecticut.

Although often exasperated, Dennis is not radically dissatisfied with Rosaleen. He was married before, as a very young man, to an English woman who died shortly after their arrival in America. But "they had never really liked each other." He feels that, on the whole, he has done not all that badly in his second marriage, with the strong, good-looking, and essentially good-natured Rosaleen.

Farm life, too, is much more tolerable for Dennis than for Rosaleen. A city-bred man, who had lived in Bristol, England, before he went to New York City, he has had all he wants of the struggles of urban existence. Moreover, growing up in England had given him the experience of exile long before he came to America. But Rosaleen, a country girl from County Sligo, feels that she never had a fair chance to exploit her youth and beauty in the glamorous activities of the city. (This, despite the fact that when it suits her purposes she pretends to distrust and disdain city people.) And she feels totally isolated among her Connecticut neighbors—the "natives," as she and Dennis call them, presumably English or Scotch Protestants, and the non-Irish immigrants, "Rooshans and Polacks and Wops no better than Black Protestants when you come right down to it."

She endlessly commiserates with herself over all the deprivations of her life, but especially over Dennis's sad decline from the fine figure of a man he was when she met him. Early in their marriage, she had given birth to a male child. But the baby had died within two days; and, apparently, she had never conceived again. Now, she treats her old and impotent husband more as a child than as a man, chastising, scolding, and coddling.

For a time, a young man named Kevin, a house painter, had made his home with them. A famous talker, as Rosaleen herself is, Kevin had been a great comfort to her. She had consciously thought of him as a kind of combination son and brother, not as a lover. And there is no evidence of any overtly improper behavior. But in the incident that preceded, and no doubt provoked, his leaving—when he showed Rosaleen a picture of the girl he had been "keeping steady" with in New York, and she put her down as a "brassy, bold-faced hussy"—the motive of sexual jealousy is obvious.

In the five years since Kevin's departure, with no word of his whereabouts, Rosaleen has suffered greatly for lack of an audience. She is an inveterate story teller, of incidents of her past life, and of her prophetic dreams. One of her favorite tales is of the death of her great-grandfather, in Ireland, when she and her sister Honora, watching over him during the last night of his life, became so engrossed in a giggling exchange of secrets about boyfriends that they forgot their duty. They were startled out of their wits when the old man suddenly sat up and with his last breath cursed them to hell. Six months later, she says, he came back in a dream to tell her that she must have a mass said to release him from Purgatory, to which he was condemned for having cursed her.

And there is the story of the Billy-cat, who disappeared for several days, and then came to her in a dream to tell how he met his death in a trap. And Dennis went to the place in the woods that the ghost cat had described and found the body. She has dreamed, too, of finding Kevin's grave, and is content thereafter that it was because he was dead that he could not let them know where he had gone rather than because he had rejected them.

Dennis is a poor listener. He has heard it all a hundred times. Besides, he is a born skeptic. Rosaleen makes the most of the occasional visits of traveling salesmen, whose business interest requires them to be attentive. And a few times she has exchanged stories with a certain rapscallion "native" neighbor of theirs. This is an aging hellion of a bachelor named Richards, who, when he is not drunk and out tearing around the countryside with his cronies, now and then stops in for a casual, front-porch visit with the O'Tooles.

But she is afraid, at the same time that she is tempted, to encourage Richards, who has shown signs of a more than neighborly interest in her. And the salesmen's visits are all too brief and infrequent. Most of the time, she has to talk either to herself or to the farm animals.

The climactic action of the story is precipitated by a dream she has that her sister Honora is dying at her home in Boston. It is the middle of a hard winter; but Rosaleen decides she must go. And the long-suffering Dennis, although he is reluctant to be left alone because he has a bad cold that might turn into pneumonia, does not try to dissuade her. More than ever, Rosaleen is a grievous mystery to him; he cannot imagine, dares not imagine, what the real purpose of the absurd trip might be. But he has learned that it is best not to cross his wife once she has made up her mind—especially on the evidence of a dream.

The next morning, she makes herself ready, as best she can before the cracked and wavery mirror that is the prime symbol of all the frustrations and disappointments of her life. The only heavy coat she has is a shabby old thing, which she is ashamed to have

Honora see. But she tells Dennis that she thinks she will take the opportunity of being in the city to buy both another coat and a new mirror.

Reaching New York City, on the first leg of her trip, she permits herself the luxury of two movies and a dish of strawberries and ice cream before boarding an overnight boat to Providence. From there, she takes another train to Boston, only to discover that Honora has moved away without leaving a forwarding address. The janitor at the apartment building offers his help. But no one can recall even having heard of an Honora Gogarty or a Mrs. Terence Gogarty. And the name is not in the telephone directory.

In a dazed whirl of emotions, rebuking herself for her folly and Honora for her callousness in not having written to tell her she was moving, Rosaleen wanders aimlessly about the cold streets. Sitting on a park bench helplessly weeping, she is joined by a thin, poorly dressed young man—a "scrap of a lad," with red hair and freckles—who strikes up a sympathetic conversation with her.

Inevitably, he reminds her of Kevin. And, momentarily forgetting her own troubles in listening to his, she invites him to lunch. His name is Hugh Sullivan, he tells her. In Ireland he had worked as an hostler at the Dublin racetracks. Now, after more than eleven months in America, he cannot find a job and is penniless.

Touched by the spectacle of his ravenous appetite, and warming to his witty good humor that no adversity has defeated, Rosaleen is so carried away that she not only slips him a ten-dollar bill but suggests that he come to Connecticut and live with her and Dennis. He deserves a good Irish home, she says, and in the farm country there should be work for a man who knows horses.

Understandably, however, Sullivan thinks that her interest in him is not entirely motherly. He has been in a "scrape" once in Dublin with a married woman like her, and wants no part of another such escapade.

She rises up in a fine fury and drives him out of the restaurant. But she is shattered by the experience. The journey back to Connecticut, even by the shortest train route, is a long and bitter one. And she has altogether forgotten her intention of buying a new coat and mirror.

By the time she gets home, she has recovered herself enough to deceive Dennis. She cheerfully lies about Honora, telling him that she has left her in good health. "She's been dangerous, but it's past." But there are more trials in store for Rosaleen.

The witless neighbor boy, who looked after Dennis while she was away, has seen a black shape on the road that he took for a demon. The tale appeals to Rosaleen's superstitious mind. She persuades the boy that he should stay overnight at their house rather than go home in the dark. In the morning, she walks home with him to explain to his mother what has happened. And, once again, she is confronted with a malicious interpretation of her charity.

The woman all but accuses her of having kept the halfwit to share her bed. "A pretty specimen you are, Missis O'Toole, with your old husband and the young boys in your house and the traveling salesmen and the drunkards lolling on your doorstep all hours."

They part with an exchange of enraged insults

and imprecations. On the way back, Rosaleen has to sit down beside the road for a time to soothe herself. Once more, she is able to put up a good front to Dennis. She tells him only that she and the neighbor woman have "exchanged the compliments of the season."

But it is clear that she is about at the end of her rope. On the train from Boston, she had thought bitterly that Kevin might have become her lover if she had not driven him away with her jealous anger. Now, she tries to take a paradoxical comfort in the realization that her dream about Honora did not come true. If that one was false, she argues with herself, then she need not believe any of them—and it follows that Kevin is not dead. But when she tells Dennis this last, and adds that she is sure Kevin will be coming to see them again, he grumpily rejects her logic. And, hearing the drunken Richards outside roaring a song from his rattling buggy, she gets up to fix her hair. Now she realizes for the first time that she has forgotten to buy the new looking-glass in Boston.

She is at least as much relieved as disappointed that Richards does not come in. The buggy stops but then starts up again after a moment. But the wild thought she has entertained for an instant, even as she started for the door to open it—how "a woman would have a ruined life with such a man, it was courting death and danger to let him set foot over the threshold"—seems to scare her at last into submission to the fate of her dull life with Dennis.

She indulges one final nostalgic review of the broken dreams of a lifetime. Then she turns, at once protecting and appealing for protection, to her old husband:

Without thinking at all, she leaned over and put her head on Dennis's knee. "Whyever," she asked him, in an ordinary voice, "did ye marry a woman like me?"

"Mind you don't tip over in that chair now," said Dennis. "I knew well I could never do better." His bosom began to thaw and simmer. It was going to be all right with everything, he could see that.

She sat up and felt his sleeves carefully. "I want you to wrap up warm this bitter weather, Dennis," she told him. "With two pairs of socks and the chest protector, for if anything happened to you, whatever would become of me in this world?"

"Let's not think of it," said Dennis, shuffling his feet.

"Let's not, then," said Rosaleen. "For I could cry if you crooked a finger at me."

Rosaleen and Dennis, in the imperfection of their union, have much in common with other married couples in Miss Porter's fiction. But the quality of the humor in "The Cracked Looking-Glass," mildly satiric and at the same time deeply affectionate, sets the story apart. It is a tone Miss Porter has struck before, but nowhere else so sustained.

The dialectal authenticity of the story, its sure control of the Irish idiom, has been widely and justly admired. But there is more than a finely tuned ear at work. The control of language embodies a deep understanding of the whole Irish-immigrant experience, in its shaping of sensibility and character. And, further, Irish-ness is an explicit and carefully developed theme in the story.

The title, as Hendrick and others have noted, is from Joyce's *Ulysses*.[1] Stephen Dedalus calls Buck Mulligan's shaving mirror, which he has stolen from a serving girl, "a symbol of Irish art. The cracked looking glass of a servant." Rosaleen has been working for fifteen years on a tablecloth that she is unlikely to finish. In the mirror and the unfinished cloth, Brother Joseph Wiesenfarth sees an allusion to Tennyson's "The Lady of Shalott."[2] And Hendrick suggests that Rosaleen's mirror is like the glass of I Corinthians 13:12.[3] But, aside from the universal values of the mirror symbol, recognizable without benefit of specific allusion, the echo of Joyce remains most immediately relevant.

Rosaleen is Irish; she was a domestic servant before her marriage, and, with the aging Dennis, has once more assumed the role. In her inveterate habit of story-telling, she is herself a type of the artist. Moreover, she is the Joycean artist-in-exile.

The holding on to the flawed mirror and the stories, about dreams come true, Rosaleen uses to the same purpose—to avoid facing the truth about herself and her situation. Her escapist tactics are not unsubtle. The hard work, her old husband's impotence, the loneliness of her exile, are harsh facts that she protests rather than denies. She is incapable of admitting that she herself might be fundamentally responsible for her fate. But she does not entertain herself with simple-minded, pleasurable fantasies. The dream stories, although they embody a claim to extrasensory powers, do not dispute the basic facts of mortality. In defiance of Dennis's skepticism, she may insist, and the more elaborately with every retelling of the story, that the Billy-cat came to her and spoke —but she never denies that the cat is dead.

When her dreams are wish fulfillment dreams, as they obviously are in the dream of Kevin's death and probably in that of Honora's illness, they are revengeful rather than pleasantly self-indulgent. Rosaleen is a proud woman, and artfully conceals her hurt and anger in images of grief and solicitude.

But she *is* hurt, of course. And when, ostensibly, she puts her dream power to the test in the trip to Boston, an adventure that Dennis obscurely senses will end disastrously, the pathetic character of her pain is so clearly revealed that even she finally cannot deny it.

Her reluctance to leave New York is undoubtedly motivated in part by her own fear that her dream will be proved untrue when she reaches Boston. But, more importantly, the way she entertains herself, with the two romantic love movies, reveals what the real purpose of the trip has been all along.

Her discovery in Boston that her sister has simply moved away, without letting her know, is disappointing and humiliating. But, to some extent, she is speaking the truth about her feelings when she tells the sympathetic janitor that "it's no great matter." She is quick enough to dry her tears when she meets Hugh Sullivan.

It is his insulting interpretation of her motives in her kindness to him—an interpretation that so infuriates her because it contains some truth—that is the truly shattering experience of the adventure in Boston. She is revealed to herself unmistakably as an aging, sexually frustrated woman, who has used the excuse of her duty to an old and impotent husband as a mask for her own sense of sexual and emotional inadequacy. The dream that has "gone back on" her, the dream in which she has now lost faith, is not so much the one of Honora's illness as it is the lifelong one of finding a young and devoted lover, who will confirm the reality of that picture of herself, of a woman of charm and beauty, that she has cherished in her imagination through the bleak years on the farm with Dennis.

On the way home, she tries to restore the dream, at least in retrospect. She persuades herself that the greatest tragedy of her life was her failure to realize that Kevin loved her and that he would have stayed if only she had asked him.

Infinitely resourceful, even after the further humiliation of the "native" neighbor's crude accusations, she is still able to turn things around. Her admission to Dennis that she no longer believes in the prophetic power of her night dreams allows her to spin new daydreams of Kevin's return. If her dream of visiting Kevin's grave is untrue, then he is alive, and, therefore, must intend soon to come back. But Dennis sourly rejects her pseudo-logic. "That's no sign at all," he says.

But when the drunken Richards comes and goes, and when she has found herself, in a moment of terrible panic, wishing that he would come in— wanting him *because* he would ruin her—she is finally stripped of all her defenses.

It occurs to her, as she hears the buggy outside and starts frantically to straighten her hair, that she forgot to buy a new looking-glass in Boston. It is clear enough why she forgot, why indeed she has put up with the flawed glass for so many years. So long as she lacks a true mirror, one that will accurately reflect her face, she can imagine herself as beautiful as she pleases. Dennis's routinely indifferent assurance that the old mirror is "good enough" is richly ironic. But it is doubtful now that she will ever again be able to deceive herself with it.

Sitting beside the road on her way back from the neighbor's house, she thought "in a soft, easy melancholy," that "life is a dream . . . a mere dream." And now, with Dennis and the cats in the kitchen, she thinks back over her life, "wondering what had become of [it]." She thinks of places she has and has not seen—"Winston and New York and Boston, and beyond that were far-off places full of life and gayety she'd never seen nor even heard of, and beyond everything like a green field with morning sun on it lay youth and Ireland like something she had dreamed, or made up in a story." But to think of *all* existence as a dream, to deny the distinction between dream and reality, is the next thing to resigning all dreams, both those of the night and those of the day.

And there is a definite suggestion of such resignation in her final words and gestures to Dennis. It is he who says, in answer to her question why he had married her—"I knew well I could never do better"— and he who thinks, "it was going to be all right with everything." But her own need and acceptance of him, as real as his need and acceptance of her, are apparent in her new solicitude for him.

One senses that she is beginning to perceive that all her romantic dreams were doubly false. It is likely that Kevin would never have become her lover, that he fled precisely because he suspected and feared her suppressed desire. But it is just as likely that she never really wanted him to be. She did not want the virile Kevin, whom if only "she had said the word" she might have kept away from the "brassy, bold-faced hussy." Rather, the Kevin she wanted, and has cherished in her idealistic memory, is the "sweet decent boy [who] would have cut off his right hand rather than give her an improper word." At an emotional level deeper than desire, the old child-man that she has, a person to be wrapped up and put to bed— the man who has taken the place of the child she lost—is the man she wanted. She too is almost ready to admit: "I knew well I could never do better."

And the reader who appreciates Miss Porter's wryly sympathetic characterization of Dennis O'Toole will agree. For all his grumbling, Dennis emerges as a remarkably tolerant and understanding man, prudent and infinitely patient with his wife, and unswervingly loyal to her, despite the capricious abuse and the embarrassment to which she repeatedly subjects him. When Dennis reproaches Rosaleen for her addiction to tall tales, and she answers complacently "that's the Irish in me," one sympathizes with Dennis's reflection that she "was always doing the Irish a great wrong by putting her own faults off on them."

Hendrick remarks: "The story ends on the same note of despair on the human condition that one finds in many of Miss Porter's other stories."[4] I think not.

The ending here is distinctly, if in a very low key, positive. Rosaleen's resignation—her resignation of her dreams, her resignation to her marriage—is distinctly, if only in a measure, an affirmation. It would be a grave critical error to sentimentalize Rosaleen's relinquishment of her dreams as cause for despair. Stephen Dedalus makes his remark about Mulligan's mirror as symbol of Irish art "with bitterness." And, if there is no bitterness here, if Miss Porter acknowledges at least a superficial charm in Rosaleen's version of that art, still there can be no doubt that she shares Stephen's fundamental critical attitude toward it. The art that Rosaleen's dreams represent—the art of illusion and self-deception, of pseudo-magic—is false art. Miss Porter's story clearly defines it as such, and clearly and firmly rejects it.

5

By Self
Possessed

In the stories that have usually been considered Miss Porter's finest work, the central figures are people whose desperate preoccupation with themselves cuts them off from effective communication with all other human beings. In some instances, a family situation, present or remembered, may be responsible for the protagonist's alienation or provide its particular dramatic circumstances. But whether the setting is a New York rooming house, where the protagonist is a long way from home and alone for most of the time of the story's action, or a Texas farmhouse, with the family present most of the time, the reader's attention is fixed upon a totally private agony.

In all but one of these stories, the protagonist is a woman. (Rosaleen O'Toole is potentially one of this type. But she retains the ability to communicate, after a fashion, with Dennis; her story is essentially comic. In its perfection, the role is tragic.) Especially in the stories about women, it may be in the failure of a sexual union that the fatal pride chiefly shows itself. But sex is ultimately of no greater importance than social class or occupation or level of literacy. What all these characters have in common, from the Miranda of "Pale Horse, Pale Rider" to Royal Earle Thompson of "Noon Wine," is a consuming devotion to some idea of themselves—of their own inestimable worth and privilege—which the circumstances of their lives do not permit them to realize in actuality but which they are powerless to abandon. The idea lives in them like a demon, directing all their thoughts and actions. Whatever it may be in which they invest that most precious and indefinable sense of self—a cherished grievance, a need to justify a fatal action, an ideal of order and mental discipline—they pursue it relentlessly, through all discomforts and deprivations, even to death—and if not to the death of the body then of the spirit, incapacitating themselves not only for love but for the enjoyment of any common good of life, to walk forever among strangers.

"María Concepción"—about a Mexican Indian girl who murders her husband's mistress and takes their baby for her own—is Miss Porter's first work in this vein. But the exotic pastoralism of that story has obscured María's character for many readers. In most interpretations, she is misrepresented as a pure primitive, who triumphs by the power of instinct over the disorder that the encroachments of alien civilization have brought to her society. As her name is surely meant to indicate, María is actually the victim of her own tragic "conceit." She commits the murder in a desperate effort to realize her obsessive idea of herself as a wife and mother—an idea that she has from her oversimplified training in Catholicism, not from her Indian heritage. In the stories having protagonists with whose North American cultural backgrounds Miss Porter, as well as her reader, is more fully and immediately familiar, the psychological and moral situations are clearer.

Theft

In keeping with the story's thematic concern, neither the heroine of "Theft," nor the city in which the action takes place, is named. But the story has a distinct autobiographical ring, and is probably based on some episode of Miss Porter's experience in New York City during the 1920s.

The protagonist, a not-so-young woman writer living alone in the city, discovers one morning that

her new purse is missing. She mentally runs through
the events of the previous evening.

She left a cocktail party with a young man
named Camilo, who walked with her to the Elevated
—with pathetic gallantry spoiling his beautiful new
biscuit-colored hat in the rain. She looked in her
purse to be sure she had the subway fare. But before
she climbed the steps, another male friend, a painter
named Roger, stopped to offer her a ride home in a
taxi. Finding that he was ten cents short on the taxi
fare, he asked her for it, and she opened her purse
for the coin. When Roger admired the purse, she told
him that it was a birthday present. She then inquired
briefly about his current show, which apparently was
not very successful.

Coming home, she accepted the invitation of
another roomer in the house to stop in for a drink.
Bill had been feeling lonely and sorry for himself
over the failure of his latest play, canceled during
rehearsal, and his ex-wife's incessant demands for
money. The protagonist offered him sympathy, but
mindful of her own poverty, she reminded him of the
fifty dollars he owed her for a part of the play she
had written. It had been agreed that she was to be
paid whatever the fate of the play. He said that he
could not give her the money, and she impulsively
told him to forget it.

Reaching her own room, she wiped off the wet
purse, and left it on a wooden bench to dry. Before
going to bed, she read over again, and then destroyed,
a letter received that day from an estranged lover.

Now, coming into the room from her bath in
search of cigarettes and unable to find the purse, she
concludes that it must have been stolen by the janitress. While she was in the bathroom, she had heard

the woman entering the apartment to check the radiators. Still in her bathrobe, she goes down to the basement, accuses the woman, and demands that she return the purse.

The janitress at first solemnly denies the accusation, swearing before God. But stung by the bitterness with which the writer responds—"keep it if you want it so much"—she follows her upstairs to confess.

She stole it on impulse, the janitress explains, for her pretty young niece. She hands over the purse, but begs forgiveness and understanding. In her explanation —that the niece "needs pretty things," that "we oughta give the young ones a chance," that the writer has "had [her] chance"—there is an implicit plea that she be allowed to keep the purse after all. Yet, when the writer tries to give it to her, saying that she no longer wants it, the janitress reverses herself and angrily refuses the purse. "I don't want it either now," she says. "My niece is young and pretty . . . I guess you need it worse than she does."

The writer reminds the janitress that the purse was not hers in the first place. "You mustn't talk as if I had stolen it from you."

But the janitress, taunting her once more with a reference to the pretty niece, has the last word: "It's not from me, it's from her you're stealing it."

Alone again, laying the recovered purse on the table and settling down to her cold cup of coffee, the writer thinks: "I was right not to be afraid of any thief but myself, who will end by leaving me nothing."

It is notable that most of the story's action is presented in recollections. Except for the two brief, direct encounters with the janitress, we see the protagonist entirely alone. And she explicitly sums up her own situation and passes judgment on herself. The technique is exactly appropriate to character and theme.

At the moment in which she bitterly tells the janitress to keep the purse,

she felt that she had been robbed of an enormous number of valuable things, whether material or intangible: things lost or broken by her own fault . . . words she had wished to hear spoken to her and had not heard, and the words she had meant to answer with; bitter alternatives and intolerable substitutes worse than nothing, and yet inescapable: the long patient suffering of dying friendships and the dark inexplicable death of love—all that she had had, and all that she had missed, were lost together, and were twice lost in this landslide of remembered losses.

She gets the purse back. But getting that one thing back as she does—with the contempt of the janitress that she recognizes as justified, since she has made a fuss over the gift without really caring about it—only confirms the general sense of spiritual loss.

At least one Shakespearean allusion is apparent. "Who steals my purse steals trash." And with a vengeance here, for, as she points out to the janitress, there is no money in it.

For the "trash" that is honest Iago's purse, the purse of mere material possessions, our heroine clearly has little regard. But the present purse, though a material object, is one of complex significance as a female sex symbol. It is beautiful, but empty. It is a gift—probably from a lover, probably the same lover whose letter, hinting at a desire for reconciliation, she read and destroyed. It is a birthday gift; thereby a reminder that to Milton's "Time, the subtle thief of youth," she has also left the door all too carelessly open. In the painful experience of the loss-recovery of the purse, the protagonist is forced to ask herself what she does value, if it is not material possessions. And the answer is terrifying.

It is not love that she wants. The letter that she so meticulously destroys is evidently an appeal for reconciliation, which she rejects. It is implied that she has had a number of lovers and is still being sought after by men. Camilo is a suitor of sorts. But the feeling elicited in her by his gesture of wearing his new hat in the rain is at best pity, at worst contempt. In her mind, she adversely compares him to a man called Eddie—perhaps the estranged husband or lover who wrote the letter she destroys—who is able to wear old and shabby hats "with a careless and incidental rightness." And watching Camilo pause to look at the hat and put it under his coat, after he leaves her at the El station, she meanly supposes that the next day he will "associate her with his misery," and regret his gallantry. She seems to be more than casually involved with Roger, who tells her in the taxi: "I had a letter from Stella today, and she'll be home on the twenty-sixth, so I suppose she's made up her mind and it's all settled." But her response, whatever else it may imply about her role in Roger's troubles with his wife, is curt and impatient. The words suggest that she is already weary of him, and probably does not care very much what he decides to do. " 'I had a sort of letter today, too,' she said, 'making up my mind for me. I think it is time for you and Stella to do something definite.' "

Her habit of leaving doors unlocked is not so much an expression of inner security, and of confidence in the goodness of humanity, as of contempt for anyone to whom material possessions are so important that he would steal. And it is contempt, and a kind of bitter indifference, not generosity, that compels her to forgive Bill's debt to her. She forgives the debt, but not the debtor.

In short, she values only herself. And she discovers by the end of the story that to love oneself, to the exclusion of all other things and persons, is ultimately to despise oneself—indeed, to lose oneself.

Her going down to the basement, in pursuit of the thieving janitress, is described in terms of a descent into the underworld. The janitress, her face smeared with soot and her eyes glowing with the fire of the furnace she is tending, is a demonic figure, accusing and threatening. And when she follows the writer back up the stairs, she still carries the infernal light in her eyes.

We are to understand that once she has glimpsed the hell of her self-imposed loneliness, the protagonist can never again escape it. It is appropriate that she should be nameless; for through her contemptuous rejections she has finally stolen from herself her very human identity.

Flowering Judas

The central character is an American schoolteacher living in Mexico. A lapsed Catholic, she has retained the attitudes and habits of mind instilled by her religious training. For the romantic piety she experienced as a Catholic, she has tried to find a new vehicle in the socialist revolution. Now she is disillusioned with the revolution, which has bogged down in petty factionalism and a corruptive struggle for power among the leaders of the various groups. But because she knows no other outlet for her deep inner need for dedication, she remains faithful to her commitment, doing her share and trying to discipline her thinking.

Laura works for the most powerful of the local revolutionary leaders, a man named Braggioni. Her job is to carry messages between him and his adherents who are in prison or hiding out to escape arrest. Braggioni is the embodiment of all the forces of corruption that threaten the revolutionary movement from within. He is a notoriously lustful man, vain, self-indulgent, ruthless, in love with power. Much to the distress of the virginal Laura, he has launched upon a determined campaign to seduce her. She would like to be rid of him; but she repeatedly reminds herself that she can do nothing for the others in her faction without his help.

As the story opens, Laura comes home at the end of the day, tired and troubled, to find Braggioni waiting for her as usual. An enormously fat man, he is wearing expensive, gaudy clothes: a lavender shirt and a purple necktie, mauve silk socks, an ammunition belt of tooled leather worked in silver. He plays his guitar—badly—and sings for her, in a strained, off-key voice. But, as always, she "listens . . . with pitiless courtesy, because she dares not smile at his miserable performance."

Laura's outfit—she is wearing a serge skirt and a severe, long-sleeved blouse with demure lace edging the high collar—is suggestive of a nun's habit. And she sits with her knees held closely together. But, incongruous with her general thinness, her breasts are very full and richly rounded.

The infatuated Braggioni, his gaze fixed on the prominent but inaccessible breasts, talks to her of love

and revolution. A dangerous time is approaching in
Morelia. The Catholics will be holding a festival of
the Blessed Virgin on the same day that the socialists
will be honoring the martyrs of the revolution. As if
inspired by the thought of the opportunity for
violence, he takes off his ammunition belt and asks
her to clean and load his pistols.

Braggioni tells Laura that he cannot understand
why she has committed herself to the revolution unless there is some man in the movement whom she
loves. She assures him there is no one she loves, and no
one who loves her. He tells her that it is her own
fault, that no woman who wants a lover need be
alone, that even "the legless beggar woman in the
Alameda has a perfectly faithful lover."

Laura does not answer. (It is well known that
several young men have tried to court her. Once
she threw a rose to a man who sang forlornly beneath her window; but even that one, small favor was
bestowed only in the hope that it would persuade
him to go away.) Gradually, Braggioni's obsessive
monologue shifts from the subject of love to violence.
He talks of the total destruction of civilization that
must come before a new and better order can evolve.

Handing him back his oiled and loaded pistols,
Laura, with uncharacteristic openness, suggests sarcas-
tically that he will feel better if he goes to Morelia
and kills somebody. As he is buckling on the belt, she
abruptly reveals the matter that has so depressed her
that evening.

A young man named Eugenio, one of Braggioni's
adherents, killed himself in prison with an overdose
of the sleeping pills Laura had taken to him. Braggioni pretends total indifference, saying that Eugenio

was a fool and they are well rid of him. But it is apparent that his mood has changed.

Leaving Laura, he goes back home to his faithful and eternally tearful wife instead of to the hotel in which he had taken refuge from her a month before. There is a grotesquely maudlin scene of reconciliation. She washes his feet and prepares his supper.

Laura, left alone, puts on her white linen nightgown and goes to bed. She is restless. When she finally does fall asleep, it is into a strange and disturbing dream.

Eugenio is calling her, to get up and follow him. Reluctantly, she follows, down the stairs and then down the Judas tree that grows beneath her window, the branches of the tree bending to let her down gently upon the earth. She continues to hold back, asking Eugenio where it is that he is taking her. At last he answers that it is to death, and that the way is long and they must hurry. She protests that she will not go unless he holds her hand. Stripping the "warm bleeding flowers" from the Judas tree, he holds them out to her in a skeletal hand, saying "take and eat." When she has greedily eaten, he calls her "murderer" and "cannibal." "This is my body and my blood," he says.

She cries out "No!" Waking herself with the cry, she is afraid to go back to sleep.

"Flowering Judas" is perhaps the best-known of Miss Porter's stories, and a great favorite of symbolist critics. In 1947, Ray West elaborately analyzed the rather elaborately obvious religious symbolism of the story.[1] Many later critics, taking West's study as a point of departure, have emphasized the erotic significance of the symbols. There are, I would agree with

practically everybody, two most important things
about Laura: she is a Catholic who has lost her faith,
and she is sexually repressed.

It hardly needs saying that the two matters have
a good deal to do with each other. The particular
kind of Catholicism, from which she has lapsed, is
that peculiarly North American, predominantly Irish,
Jansenist cult—historically competitive with the earlier
established tradition of Protestant puritanism in the
United States—which makes religion all but exclusively
a matter of morality, and morality all but exclusively
sex morality. The ideal of sexual "purity" is the basis
of all other idealisms.

For the person cast in this mold (whether offi-
cially lapsed or unlapsed), dirty, sensual Mexico
(whether Catholic or socialist) exercises the ultimate
charm of attraction-repulsion, offers the ultimate
test of puritan idealism. Desperate sometimes because of
her inability to sustain the inner conviction of her
revolutionary commitment, Laura pays clandestine
visits to churches. Thus she briefly and unsuccessfully
tries to revive at least the emotion of her dead faith.
The Roman Catholic Church in Mexico depended
upon its alliance with the hereditary landowners for
its wealth and political power and secured its hold on
the minds of the common people through perpetua-
tion of what the socialists regarded as superstitious
beliefs and practices, such as those involved in the
cult of the Blessed Virgin, the veneration of the Saints,
and the Eucharistic sacrifice. It was regarded as one of
the greatest enemies of the revolutionary movement.
And Laura is acutely aware that simply by entering
a church she is suspect as a traitor to the revolutionary
cause. But it is not primarily on account of any
pang of socialist conscience, not because she is no

longer able to *believe*, rationally, in the doctrines of Roman Catholicism, that Laura fails in her efforts to revive the emotions of her earlier faith. Her recitation of the rosary is "no good," simply because she cannot suppress her furtive and deliciously guilty, erotic reaction to her physical surroundings:

. . . she ends by examining the altar with its tinsel flowers and ragged brocades, and feels tender about the battered doll-shape of some male saint whose white, lace-trimmed drawers hang limply around his ankles below the hieratic dignity of his velvet robe.

The delicate fetishism of her love of fine lace, which distracts her here from her religious devotions, makes her also, in her own eyes, a "heretic" to the revolutionary faith. She cherishes a drawerful of dainty collars, all edged with handmade lace. " . . . she will not wear lace made on machines. This is her private heresy, for in her special group the machine is sacred, and will be the salvation of the workers."

The flaw that effects Laura's alienation from the church is the same flaw that prevents her from being a wholehearted revolutionist. The fault is not difficult to define. The lace of her collars, wrapped in blue tissue paper and laid away in a drawer, or worn high around her neck as a delicate armor against improper advances, symbolizes the desperate privacy of her eroticism. To the extent that she is even aware of her erotic impulses for what they are, she has been unable to reconcile them to her ideal of community faith, whether religious or sociopolitical.

The grossly sensual, vainly self-indulgent Braggioni, whose name defines his character, represents a corruption and betrayal of the humanitarian ideals of the revolution. A "professional lover of humanity," he has nothing but contempt for most men, even his fawning followers, and takes his greatest delight in killing people. His wretched wife's washing his feet, a grotesque parody of Mary's act of obeisance to Jesus (John 12:3), emphasizes with heavy irony Braggioni's falsity both in the role of repentant and forgiving husband and in that of his people's savior.

But Laura, too, has served him humbly. In the description of her dutiful submission to his request that she clean and oil his pistols, the phallic symbolism of the guns is overt. She will not sleep with Braggioni, but her fondling of the deadly weapons is, if anything, more obscene.

Laura, in truth, is no less the "professional lover of humanity" than Braggioni, her high-minded frigidity no less inhumane than his cruel sensuality. The Indian children she teaches are evidently very fond of her—covering her desk with fresh flowers every day, and on one occasion inscribing in colored chalks on the blackboard the words "We lov ar ticher"—but there is no indication that she responds with any warmth even to this innocent affection or has willingly done anything to inspire it. The teaching is a tiresome duty, like all the other tasks she performs in the abstract interest of the revolution.

The dream she has after Braggioni leaves makes it clear that Eugenio had been trying to seduce her. She had evidently felt strongly attracted to him. But to help him to sleep she had given him narcotics, not herself; and she obviously suspects that he took the overdose because he had lost hope of winning her love, not because of despair at his continuing imprisonment. That her dream of him awakens her and makes her afraid to go back to sleep is ironically appropriate to what she has done in giving him the narcotics, affording him a sleep from which he will never awaken.

From Braggioni's point of view, Eugenio's suicide is a betrayal, although not a very important one, of the revolutionary cause. Laura subconsciously attempts to convince herself of this view in her dream-identification of Eugenio with the Judas tree; his flesh and blood are the blossoms of the tree, its twigs the fingerbones of his skeletal hands. (In legend, it was from the redbud, or Judas tree, that Christ's betrayer hanged himself.) But in eating the flowers, she acknowledges herself as the traitor, and Eugenio after all as the Son of Man.

The dream's mock communion, with the body and blood of Judas substituted for that of Christ, might be seen as embodying Laura's suppressed conviction that her association with the revolutionary movement is a betrayal of her first Lord. Or the imagery will as easily support an opposite interpretation. Perhaps Laura feels guilty about her continuing, furtive flirtations with Catholicism, seeing them as a betrayal of the revolutionary cause. It is for this that Eugenio condemns her in the dream with the words "murderer" and "cannibal"—which are such words as a good socialist might use for Catholic communicants. But the important thing, either way, is that she has betrayed herself, her own humanity, in her refusal to love.

Her refusing in the dream to accompany Eugenio on the journey to death unless he will take her hand is a gesture of ambiguous significance. It is at once an acknowledgment of her need for love, and a sign of her continuing reluctance to admit it. When Eugenio finally extends his hand, it is the bony hand of death, one proferring a substance that is the food of death, not life.

Laura is afraid to go back to sleep, perhaps to reenter the dream, because she has recognized there the falsity of *all* her communions. She had gone to sleep silently repeating to herself that "it is monstrous to confuse love with revolution." But, as she senses in the dream, it is precisely in failing to achieve that confusion, or fusion, that she betrays every cause that requires her loyalty.

The point is that there is no true religion, and no true revolution, without love. The puritan mind that regards the inevitable "confusions" of the human condition—"love with revolution, night with day, life with death," spirit with body—as "monstrous" must end with making a monster of man himself. It is just this that Laura makes of Eugenio and of herself—he becoming the walking tree-skeleton, she the cannibal murderer who eats of his not-flesh. The cry of "No!" with which she awakens herself would deny her self-conviction of inhumanity. But we recognize it also as a despairing repetition of the cry with which, in the reality of waking experience, she has met all demands for human involvement. She is still bound to the lifelong habit of denial, or rejection, that has led her to the monstrous confrontation in the dream.

Pale Horse, Pale Rider

The heroine of "Pale Horse, Pale Rider" is Miranda at the age of twenty-four. No longer married, six years after the time of her conversation with

Cousin Eva at the end of "Old Mortality," she is working for a Denver newspaper as drama critic. The time is 1918, near the end of World War I. The influenza epidemic is at its height. On her salary of eighteen dollars a week, Miranda is barely able to maintain a respectable existence. She is nevertheless being constantly badgered by Liberty Bond salesmen to pledge five of the eighteen to the glorious cause.

Totally disenchanted with a job to which she was not so much appointed as relegated, because she had showed herself lacking the emotional toughness believed indispensable for a news reporter, Miranda has little conscious incentive for maintaining the wearying routine of existence. She is induced to join a group of women visiting an army hospital, with gifts of flowers and candy and cigarettes for the patients. Out of instinctive sympathy for his very aloofness, in the self-isolation of physical and mental pain, she chooses an especially somber patient to talk to. But he will not answer or so much as look at the basket she has placed on his bed. She leaves with the sick determination never to attempt such a visit again.

A play she is attending is interrupted for an unannounced speech of patriotic exhortation by one of the local dollar-a-year men. She feels assaulted by the tawdry clichés—"These vile Huns—glorious Belleau Wood—our keyword is Sacrifice—Martyred Belgium—give till it hurts—our noble boys Over There—Big Berthas—the death of civilization—the Boche." In response she silently cries out: "Coal, oil, iron, gold, international finance, why don't you tell us about them, you little liar?"

Bill, her boss on the newspaper, is a living caricature, "exactly like city editors in the moving pictures, even to the chewed cigar." Her friend Chuck Rouncivale, the "hardboiled and professional" sportswriter, is in reality a profoundly insecure man, feeling obliged constantly to apologize for the bad lung that keeps him out of the war, which he cynically pretends to despise. She is stubbornly conscientious about her work as critic. But when a traveling actor, a seedy has-been, whom she has panned, shows up at the office to protest—displaying a sheaf of yellowed press clippings about his past successes in the big cities and making teary-eyed threats—she can feel nothing except a desperate embarrassment. Her job suddenly seems to her worse than pointless, and she wants only to get away from the pathetic little man as quickly as possible.

She falls in love with a young engineering officer from Texas, who has quite by chance taken a room in the house where she lives. Adam is the embodiment of ideal masculinity—earthily handsome, strong physically and emotionally, sympathetic, easily affectionate, intelligently simple, uncynically realistic. But very early in their acquaintance, Miranda has a premonition that Adam is destined to die young. Her love for him, the vision of sane and creative life that it offers her in the midst of the shabby bad dream of her routine existence, is to turn out the greatest sham of all.

On the day she and Adam first openly acknowledge their love, Miranda contracts influenza. Because of the epidemic, hospital space is not readily available, and for a few days Adam looks after her in the rooming house. Finally he does succeed in getting her into a hospital, shortly before his outfit is transferred.

For several weeks she hovers between life and death, in a shadowy state of recurrent delirium in which it is difficult to distinguish between dream and waking reality. Then, surviving the critical phase, she recovers full consciousness on the day the armistice is announced.

Several days later, when she is strong enough to go through the bundle of letters that have been saved for her, she comes on one in an unfamiliar handwriting that tells her Adam is dead—of influenza. The writer explains that he had promised to let Miranda know "in case anything happened."

For a time, Miranda is unable to reconcile herself to the fact of Adam's death, which it seems to her makes an intolerable "cheat" of her own effort to come back to life. She talks to him in her mind. Once she conjures his ghost, pleading with him to let her see him once more. But at last she sternly rejects such fantasies, determining that she will face unflinchingly the reality of her lonely future.

The essential action of "Pale Horse, Pale Rider" is easily summarized, and the summary could lead one to suspect that this novella depends too heavily on coincidence for its dramatic impact. But the narrative technique is more subtle and more complex than in any other of Miss Porter's stories. The exact chronological sequence of events is difficult, at times almost impossible, to determine. Past and present, night and day, dream and waking, the world of the mind and the world of the senses, are interfused—seldom, and never for more than moments, to be distinguished. The center of interest is in Miranda's consciousness, in her subjective responses rather than in the actions in which she is objectively involved.

The pervasive sense of "unreality" that Miss Porter creates with image and rhythm, with mis-

chievous settings and resettings of the narrative clock,
is appropriate to the abnormal state of mind in her
protagonist that can be circumstantially accounted
for. Miranda experiences, only more intensely, we
must suppose, than most people, the universal
paranoia of wartime. Her job on the newspaper requires her to keep "what she had been brought up to
believe were unnatural hours, eating casually at dirty
little restaurants, drinking bad coffee all night, and
smoking too much." And, finally, she is sick. The first
symptoms of her near-fatal illness are apparent in the
opening episode of the story, her troubled waking
from the dream of a horseback ride in the company of
a sinister stranger.

But technique and circumstance are also intimately related to theme. The novella is *about* appearance and reality. And the question it poses is whether
that which at first appears to be abnormal, unreal,
in Miranda's experience, may not in fact be the most
profound reality.

Miranda, here as in all the stories about her, is
the nonconformist. Not conspicuously, dramatically
so; not even very confidently or courageously. The
"irregularities" of her life style are minor. She recognizes the practical advantages of conformity, and is
not sure but what she will, after all, sign up for the
Liberty Bond rather than risk losing her job, and the
meager income it provides. In her mind, she cries out
"liar" to the patriotic speaker at the theater. But she
is cautious about what she says to even the friendliest
of her fellow journalists, Chuck Rouncivale and the
gossip columnist Mary "Towney" Townsend. She is
completely open only with Adam. Yet, however diffi-
dently, however much she might even *like* to buy,

not only the Bond, but the solidarity with her society that it represents, she refuses to submit any more than necessary either to the inward or to the outward pressures. However quietly and haltingly, she marches to a different drum.

Like many another protagonist in modern literature, Miranda is much preoccupied with time. The voices and signs of chronological time, clock-time, are associated in the story with the regulations and pieties, the value structures, of the political and economic society. At the beginning, struggling out of sleep and her disturbing dream, she hears the word *war* "strike" in her mind like a gong—"a gong of warning, reminding her for the day long what she forgot happily in sleep, and only in sleep. The war, said the gong, and she shook her head." At the end, awakening from the long sleep of her illness to a cacophony of bells, she is told by the nurse that the uproar is in celebration of the armistice. But whether to remind her that the war is still going on, or to tell her that it has ended, the message of these "hammer strokes of metal tongues" is always essentially the same for malingering Miranda. The tolling is the intrusive voice of social responsibility, demanding that she rise up from her dream of death and take her place in the nightmare of life.

To the demands of public time, Miranda opposes those of the *durée réel* of her personal consciousness. This time, and her determination to remain privately loyal—however she may act publicly—to the vision her terrible submission to it provides, are symbolized in the stockings without clocks that she wants for the wardrobe of her resurrection.[2] On the day she is to leave the hospital:

Miranda, sitting up before the mirror, wrote carefully:
"One lipstick, medium, one ounce flask Bois d'Hiver perfume, one pair of gray suede gauntlets without straps, two
pairs gray sheer stockings without clocks—"

Towney, reading after her, said, "Everything without
something so that it will be almost impossible to get?"

"Try it though," said Miranda, "they're nicer without. . . ."

The society of the newspaper people is superficially liberated, and liberal. Working while others
sleep, sleeping while others work, they affect a
bohemian carelessness and cynicism about patriotism
and all bourgeois pieties. But, in truth, the night they
turn into day is regulated by the same clock that
governs the system they pretend to despise. The
newspaper is designed to serve the system.

The self-defensive Chuck Rouncivale, who,
Miranda sees, is like all the other men who have been
rejected for military service—"War was the one thing
they wanted, now they couldn't have it"—knows
very well how the economic machinery works and
urges her to adapt to it. Trying to console her after
the depressing interview with the broken-down actor,
he advises her to "toughen up."

Forget that fellow. . . . All you have to do is play up the
headliners, and you needn't even mention the also-rans.
Try to keep in mind that Rypinsky has got show business
cornered in this town; please Rypinsky and you'll please
the advertising department, please them and you'll get a
raise.

But the wisdom of such easy cynicism is against her
nature. " 'I seem to keep learning all the wrong
things,' said Miranda hopelessly."

Nance and other critics have found the characterization of Adam shallow and unconvincing.[3] It is impossible to say whether Miss Porter meant, and failed, to give him credibility as a flesh-and-blood lover. But his function in the story as it stands is clear enough. He represents, as opposed to her newspaper friends, Miranda's last and best hope for accommodating her personal needs to the demands of society.

Adam speaks her language. She can "be herself" with him, reveal her truest feelings, as in her outrage against the patriotic speaker at the theater, without fear of rebuke. And yet this man, whose personality is so beautifully responsive to hers, is at the same time capable of accommodating to the system.

Without rejecting Miranda and her feelings, sharing her embarrassment over the speech and her contempt for the superpatriot, he attains a transcendent tolerance that cools her anger.

Adam turned eyes of genuine surprise upon her. "Oh, *that* one," he said. "Now what could the poor sap do if they did take him? It's not his fault," he explained, "he can't do anything but talk."

Adam is unabashedly all-American. Books, except for engineering textbooks, bore him. He loves things he can get his hands on. Automobiles, airplanes, machinery of all kinds. For art, "things carved out of wood or stone." Confident in his unaffected masculinity, he is "nearly used to" even the wristwatch that he must wear as part of the standard military equipment, although like all provincial American boys of his generation he had been brought up to regard wristwatches as "sissy." He does not love the war, does not need it, as many do, as an escape from the intolerable problems of peace. But, with unheroic and earnest matter-of-factness, he accepts it as his duty to fight. The uniform symbolic of that duty is "as tough and unyielding in cut as a strait jacket"; he is "infinitely buttoned, strapped, harnessed" into it. But he has cheerfully made the most that can be made of it, with a "cloth that was fine and supple" and "the best tailor he could find."

And for a time Miranda is almost persuaded, allowing herself to hope that in Adam something *can* be made of civilization, specifically of American civilization, after all. In Adam we have a fairly obvious embodiment of the notorious American dream. Very briefly, Miranda is ready to believe that that dream can be redeemed, if necessary even by the hated war—that it is worth redeeming if it can command the loyalty of such as Adam.

But this hope is blasted almost as soon as it is born. Admiring Adam as he walks along, talking about the "poor sap" who made the speech at the theater, she thinks how "his pride in his youth, his forbearance and tolerance and contempt for that unlucky being breathed out of his very pores as he strolled, straight and relaxed in his strength."

But she is soon to realize that the strength, the forbearance, the beautiful and tolerant self-confidence of Adam, is a function *only* of his youth. Later, he waits for her in a coffeeshop while she goes to the office to write a review. When she returns, in the moment before he sees her, she catches a brief glimpse of his unguarded face: "an extraordinary face, smooth and fine and golden in the shabby light, but now set in a blind melancholy, a look of pained suspense and disillusion." She sees that the war has already started to kill his youth, his mind and spirit of youth. "For just one split second she got a glimpse of Adam when he would have been older, the face of the man he would not live to be." The glimpse is a premonition of his physical death. But, what is even more important, it is a glimpse of the truth that the Adam of her hope, the youthful Adam, is already as good as dead.

The world is forever soiled, rotten. Power corrupts. Innocence—the innocence of Adam, of the youthful America he represents, of the American Dream—has too little strength to survive.

Abandoning the hope that Adam brought to her, Miranda enters upon the dark journey of her nightmare-ridden illness in quest of the wisdom that will enable her to survive. Idealist that she is, the beautiful dream being impossible, she wants to die with Adam. But the death wish is repeatedly denied in her bad dreams. At the level of her subconscious, she does not, in fact, want to die.

This is first apparent in the dream with which the story opens. The dream setting is the house of her childhood, and Death appears to her in the figure of a "lank greenish stranger," with a gray horse, whom she has seen hanging about the house. Although he is a stranger, she knows that she has seen him somewhere before, and that he means to accompany her on her morning ride. But the horse she decides to take, Graylie, is chosen "because he is not afraid of bridges"—an allusion to the superstition that evil spirits cannot cross a running stream. She intends, as she says to her horse, to "outrun Death and the Devil." At the end of the dream, she tells the stranger to leave her and ride on; and he does, without looking back.

Later, when she is helplessly sick, and Adam is

taking care of her, she has a dream in which she sees
him in a jungle being repeatedly struck by flights of
arrows. Each time he is struck down, he miraculously
rises up, only to be felled again. At length, in an impulse of protective jealousy, she throws herself in
front of him, to take the arrows into her own body.
But they pass through her and again strike Adam,
this time to kill him.

The familiar symbolic association of death with
the experience of sexual climax—such an association as
is embodied in the commonplace ambiguity of the
word "die" in Elizabethan poetry—is involved here.
Miranda wants to "die" with Adam in the erotic
sense; but her dream expresses her fear that one or
both of them will actually die before their love can
be consummated. (Compare, for example, the situation
in *Romeo and Juliet*.) Hendrick sees a phallic symbolism in the arrows and the image of Adam's repeated rising and falling.[4] Miranda's intentions in the
"protective" gesture of throwing herself in front of
Adam are ambivalent; perhaps the dream gives covert
expression to her repressed feelings of female envy of
the male. But the dream is primarily relevant to
Miranda's thoughts and feelings about actual death.
Her superficial desire, which is that of dying with
Adam, or in his stead, protecting him, is at work in
the dream as well as in her conscious thoughts. But
the final outcome of the dream action plainly fulfills
her truer and deeper wish, *not* to die.

It seems to Miranda, stunned and exhausted by
her long illness and the loss of Adam, that her friends
and the doctor and nurse have entered into a kind of
"conspiracy"—absurdly cruel, totally inexplicable—to
drag her wasted and unwilling body back into life.

Miranda's fevered and tormented imagination

works on the German name of her doctor, Hildes-
heim, to make him into a figure of monstrous evil,
destroyer rather than deliverer. Rationally, she has
always rejected the stereotype of the German created
by the war propagandists—the Boche, the Hun, the
soldier with the baby impaled on his bayonet. But
the caricature has lodged itself at a deeper level of
consciousness, and merges with other images that
survive from the fearful fantasies of childhood to
form the menacing figure of the "executioner" in
white who stands beside her bed. On recovering consciousness, painfully embarrassed at the memory of the
foul words she shouted at him in her delirium, she
apologizes to the doctor. Still there is a sense in
which he remains for her a malign figure. For what is
it, she asks herself, that "the whole humane conviction and custom of society" has "conspired" to do
except to "set her once more safely in the road that
would lead her again to death"?

It will simply "not do," she tells herself, "to
betray the conspiracy and tamper with the courage of
the living; there is nothing better than to be alive,
everyone has agreed on that; it is past argument, and
who attempts to deny it is justly outlawed." The
bitter irony is obvious. And yet there is a truth of
conviction in her final mood of resignation to the
conspiracy, her *joining* it, indeed, that is beyond
irony.

In the final dream-vision of her illness, Miranda
discovers in herself an indestructible will to live:

Death is death, said Miranda. . . . Silenced she sank easily
through deeps under deeps of darkness until she lay like a
stone at the farthest bottom of life . . . and there remained
of her only a minute fiercely burning particle of being
that knew itself alone, that . . . set itself unaided to resist

destruction, to survive and be in its own madness of being. . . . Trust me, the hard unwinking angry point of light said. Trust me, I stay.

Briefly, a heavenly vision of tranquil beauty is generated out of the burning particle:

At once it grew, flattened, thinned to a fine radiance . . . through which Miranda, enchanted, altogether believing, looked upon a deep clear landscape of sea and sand, of soft meadow and sky, freshly washed and glistening with transparencies of blue. . . . Moving towards her . . . came a great company of human beings, and Miranda saw in an amazement of joy that they were all the living she had known. Their faces were transfigured, each in its own beauty . . . and she moved among them . . . and each figure was alone but not solitary.

The happy enchantment is soon broken:

Miranda felt without warning a vague tremor of apprehension . . . ; something, somebody, was missing. . . . There are no trees, no trees here, she said in fright, I have left something unfinished. . . . Where are the dead? We have forgotten the dead, oh, the dead, where are they? At once as if a curtain had fallen, the bright landscape faded, she was alone in a strange stony place of bitter cold . . . calling out, Oh, I must go back! But in what direction?

And she awakens to a sickening stench of corruption that, after a moment, she recognizes as coming from her own body.

But, it is clearly implied, the hard faith of the first vision does endure. The "fiery motionless particle," the "hard unwinking angry point of light" that is the simple will "to survive and to be in its own madness of being" is not quenched.

It is a faith without joy, without the sentiment of charity, a faith in which the social impulses are reduced to a bitterly good-humored tolerance. We have come a long way from the ending of "Old Mortality," and Miranda's making promises to herself "in her hopefulness, her ignorance." Hope, too, is gone now, along with the ignorance upon which it depended. For the Miranda of "Pale Horse, Pale Rider," to entertain hope would be to deny the knowledge of death that is synonymous with her faith.

To the orthodox Christian mind, such faith—faith without hope and charity—is insupportable. And, again, it would be a mistake to completely identify Miranda with Miss Porter. But there is no blinking the fact that such is the faith Miss Porter attributes to her protagonist—and that the attribution is made with total artistic integrity. The gray Miranda of the ending here—Miranda ordering gray gloves without straps and gray stockings without clocks, Miranda this reluctant Lazarus—is the only Miranda the story will yield.

The Jilting of Granny Weatherall

The Southern family of this story is very much like Miranda's family—which is to say, like the Porter family. Ellen Weatherall, the "Granny" of the title, is a character strikingly similar to Sophia Jane, the grandmother in "Old Mortality" and in the stories of *The Old Order*. But here there is no one like Miranda, whose consciousness dominates the other, clearly autobiographical stories; and Miss Porter uses a narrative technique that permits her to identify much more directly with Mrs. Weatherall than she ever does with Sophia Jane.

The old woman is dying, in the house of one of
her daughters. The actual events of the day—the
morning visit of a doctor, who carries on a whispered
conversation with the daughter; the daughter's com-
ings and goings during the following hours; the
gathering of the doctor and all Mrs. Weatherall's
living children at her bedside in the evening, with the
priest who comes to administer last rites—are confused in her failing consciousness with episodes of
her past life.

People and things escape their identities. She con-
fuses the living daughter with one presumably long
since dead. The sound of the whispered conversation
between the daughter and the doctor becomes in her
mind the rustling of leaves, then of newspapers. The
lamp beside her bed becomes the light of her own
consciousness, her life; at the end of the story she
watches the lamp diminish and fade. She loses her
sense of the progression of time on this day, as well as
in her recollection of all the past days and years—
when the doctor returns in the evening, she thinks it
has been only a few minutes since he left in the
morning. Her sense of place too is confused. The
room in which she lies becomes the room in which she
awaited her bridegroom, that in which she bore her
last child. Searching for that daughter, she rises in
her mind to move through many rooms. The fields
and the roads invade the house, and she is riding in
the rough cart that is the voice of her attendant
daughter.

From the stream-of-consciousness account, given
in the third person by the omniscient author, it is not
difficult to reconstruct the principal events of Ellen
Weatherall's life. Her first fiancé, George, never ar-
rived for the wedding, and, it would seem, was never

heard from again. Later, she married another man, John, with whom she had a brief but happy life, bearing him five children. He died when he was a comparatively young man. Her widowed life, with the children to raise and the farm to look after, was hard. An energetic and competent woman, she survived illnesses and all other adversities to see her children grow up into responsible and relatively prosperous adults.

At the age of sixty, she had a premonition of death, which she prepared for by making a series of visits to her children, which she thought would be the last. She recovered from the severe fever that followed, to live another twenty years. But the experience left her with a serene assurance that she would never again fear death. On her last day, she refuses until just before the end to admit that she is gravely ill, but she acts in this way more from impatience at the fussy attentions of the daughter and doctor and priest than from fear. Still the same strong-willed, toughly humorous matriarch she has always been, she looks back on her life with great self-satisfaction.

Yet, her end is not entirely untroubled. When she begins to face the fact that she is dying, she is distressed by the thought of all the undone things—household tasks planned but not completed, details of her will not clearly stated. "I meant to do something about the Forty Acres, Jimmy doesn't need it and Lydia will later on, with that worthless husband of hers." More deeply, she is disturbed by the absence of her youngest child, a daughter called Hapsy, who, it is implied, died as a young woman shortly after giving birth to a child. The facts are obscure. Perhaps Hapsy never had the baby. But the dying woman repeatedly calls for Hapsy, and at times imagines that she is there in the room, holding the baby in her arms—or standing beside the bed in a nurse's uniform.

Finally, the old woman is tormented by the realization that she has not conquered her bitterness against George, the man who jilted her. After sixty years of unrelenting effort to convince herself that she has overcome her anger and resentment, an effort made out of the conviction that not to overcome her feelings was to condemn herself to hell, her mind in the last moment of life is filled with the grief of that betrayal.

Watching the seemingly flickering and dwindling light of the blue-shaded lamp on the bedside table, she cries out in her soul asking God to "give a sign." But—

For the second time there was no sign. Again no bridegroom and the priest in the house. She could not remember any other sorrow because this grief wiped them all away. Oh, no, there's nothing more cruel than this—I'll never forgive it. She stretched herself with a deep breath and blew out the light.

Granny Weatherall's name is probably the most obvious example of characterization by word-play in Miss Porter's fiction. The old lady has weathered all in her time—except, of course, the grief of the jilting. And the broad humor of the name's appropriateness is carried out in the whole technique of the story. The wry comedy that dominates the beginning reappears frequently and unpredictably thereafter, almost if not quite to the end. It starts off with Granny's crotchety observations on the pretentious bedside manner of "young" (actually middle-aged) Doctor Harry: "The brat ought to be in knee breeches. Doctoring around the country with spectacles on his nose! 'Get along now, take your schoolbooks and go. There's nothing wrong with me.'" When the priest is administering the last rites, her mind wanders, and for an instant she responds mentally to his touch with absurd, arch prudery:

Father Connolly murmured Latin in a very solemn voice and tickled her feet. My God, will you stop that nonsense. I'm a married woman.

But the comedy here is very near to hysteria. And we see that the intent of it, all along, is to prepare for the unsentimental, high pathos of the ending. William Nance has justly observed that Granny Weatherall is one of Miss Porter's most sympathetic characters, and that her humor is a principal means by which she is made sympathetic.[5] But Mrs. Weatherall's story is finally a very grim one; we are only the more impressed with the terror of a grief that could defeat so comic a spirit.

The mysterious figure of Hapsy[6]—whom I take to be the last of her children, who "should have been born first, for it was the one she had truly wanted," and for whom she is still searching as the others gather about her deathbed ("It was Hapsy she really wanted")—is named as an embodiment of the happiness that has eluded her all her life. In her good husband and children, her dutiful and useful life, she has rational cause for contentment. But the pleasure of her recollections during this last day of her life, at first marred only by fretfulness over trifling tasks left undone, is gradually undercut by a recurrent, terrifying sense of something lost, or missed, something that she can never quite define, something so important that the lack of it makes all that she had as nothing.

In one of her hallucinations, Hapsy appears to her in something of archetypal guise, the image of the Great Mother—probably, in Mrs. Weatherall's Catholic-trained imagination, a figure having associations with that of the Blessed Mother, or of Anne, the mother of the Virgin Mary. Hapsy is holding a baby in her arms. And Granny "seemed to herself to be Hapsy also, and the baby on Hapsy's arm was Hapsy and himself and herself, all at once, and there was no surprise in the meeting." Hapsy recognizes and greets her, and tells her that she "hasn't changed a bit." Clearly, the meeting is a vision of her anticipated reunion with Hapsy in heaven. But just as they are about to kiss, the voice of the living Cornelia penetrates her consciousness to ask "Is there anything I can do for you?" and the apparition of Hapsy is gone. In her mind, Mrs. Weatherall answers Cornelia to say that "Yes . . . she would like to see George. I want you to find George. Find him and be sure to tell him I forgot him."

The irony of her "forgetting" is obvious. And, rather obviously, the vision of bliss in the meeting with Hapsy—embodying as it does Mrs. Weatherall's egotistic and all but exclusively maternal idea of happiness—falls considerably short of heavenly perfection. In the vision, the only male figure, even momentarily recognizable as such, is the baby, in whom the images of Hapsy's baby and of the infant Jesus are merged. And the old woman identifies herself not only with the mother but also with the child.

Nance has rightly defined the essential frigidity of Ellen Weatherall, the tendency that she has in common with so many of Miss Porter's heroines to emasculate her men, to reduce them to children.[7] John, it is clear, was accepted not as a lover but only as a necessary biological instrument of her maternal instinct. And the children she would keep as children. She is proud that her son George (named, oddly enough, for the truant bridegroom) still runs to her, his eighty-year-old mother, for financial advice. Not only the doctor but also the priest, the "Father," is treated like a bumptiously playful boy.

But the sexual syndrome begins to take on metaphysical, and theological, implications when we realize that she wants the whole world, all the things of time and space and beyond, to yield to her mother-housekeeper's need for tidiness and predictability. (The missing Hapsy is troublesome to her also as "hap," circumstance, the fortuitous event, all the things that merely happened, which were not laid out in her plan.) With the clean linen of her rage for order, she will make up the rumpled bed of the universe before she dies—"thank God there was always a little margin left over for peace: then a person could spread out the plan of life and tuck in the edges orderly. It was good to have everything clean and folded away."

"For the second time there was no sign. Again no bridegroom and the priest in the house." Although the priest is there, and this time duly performs the sacred ritual, the second bridegroom, the Christ of Matthew 25:1–13, does not come. In a sense he denies her his presence for the same reason that George did —which is that He knows she does not really want Him. She wants no one, and nothing, that she cannot completely control. It is too much for her to accept that the Blessed Mother should have to yield to the Son of Man. She blows out the light of life herself, rather than let Him do it.

And yet, for all that, she does want a bridegroom—and has him, perhaps, at last. Earlier, she has
regarded Cornelia's blue silk-shaded lamp contemptu-
ously as "no sort of light at all, just frippery." "You
had to live forty years with kerosene lamps to appreciate honest electricity." But Cornelia's lamp—either
an oil lamp or a lamp with the bulb shaded to dim
and soften it—is not designed for reading or sewing
or any of the tasks for which "honest electricity" is
better. It is a light for the marriage bed. And in the
end Ellen accepts that same light as the light of life
itself. That common thing, the sexual satisfaction that
her daughter presumably has had in this bedroom, is
after all the dying woman's deepest desire. And I
suggest that when she stretches herself to blow it out,
the act is one not of final defiance but of final sur-
render—to welcome to her bed the *third* bridegroom.

The story is replete with literary allusions. Hendrick has noted, among the Shakespearean echoes, the
similarity of Cornelia's name to that of Lear's faithful daughter. He has also suggested an extended
parallel of "The Jilting of Granny Weatherall" to
Henry James's "The Beast in the Jungle."[8] But the
man who mounts the jolting cart of Cornelia's voice,
to take the reins from Ellen when she would have
driven it herself, the man whom she recognizes although she does not look at his face,[9] the man to
whom she has yielded her will then, and whom she
awaits, I believe, in the darkness at the end, should
be most familiar to us as the speaker's companion in
a poem by another American woman, Emily Dickin-
son:

> Because I could not stop for Death
> He kindly stopped for me . . .

Noon Wine

The story of "Noon Wine," with a relatively uncomplicated plot, covers the events of nine years in the life of a family on a small South Texas farm at the turn of the century. On a hot late-summer day in 1896, the owner of the farm—a "tough weather-beaten . . . noisy proud man" named Thompson, Mr. Royal Earle Thompson—is approached by a stranger looking for work.

Accustomed to expecting the worst of all hired help, the lazy, shrewd Mr. Thompson agrees to take the man on at wages of seven dollars a month, plus lodging, and meals at the family table. The stranger, a Mr. Olaf Helton, says that he earned a dollar a day in the wheat fields of North Dakota, but accepts Thompson's offer without quibbling.

Mr. and Mrs. Thompson soon discover the real bargain they have got in Helton. He is punctual, hard-working, frugal, and efficient. He methodically tidies up the operations of the farm, which the ramshackly Thompson, blaming fate and his wife's chronic sickliness, has allowed to fall into deplorable disorder.

Helton is dour and taciturn, keeping to himself in his leisure hours, and seems to take no pleasure in anything except the lonely music he makes with his remarkable collection of harmonicas. (The title of the story refers to the theme of his favorite tune—a Scandinavian drinking song, the Thompsons are to learn later, about a farmworker who improvidently drinks up during the morning the bottle of wine he brought to the fields to have with his lunch.) From time to time, Mrs. Thompson makes a timid effort to bring him out of himself but is always rebuffed.

Once a mild family crisis develops over Helton's strangely violent reaction to the Thompson children's sneaking into his shack to try out the harmonicas. Mrs. Thompson is disturbed when she sees him shaking the frightened boys in a cold and silent fury. But both she and her husband are too sensible of Helton's economic value, as well as anxious about their offspring's delinquent tendencies, to take sides against the hired man. They are troubled by the incident, but stand behind Helton. And, as the years go by, and the farm becomes more and more profitable under his management, Mr. Thompson from time to time rewards him with an unsolicited raise.

Then, on another summer afternoon, reminiscent of the first nine years before, but even more mercilessly hot, still, and dry, a second stranger arrives at the Thompsons' gate. There is something oddly and unpleasantly disconcerting about the man, for all his outward joviality, something indefinably sinister. He identifies himself as Mr. Homer T. Hatch, and, after a good deal of joke-cracking and random fat-chewing, tells Thompson that he has come to inquire about Olaf Helton.

The farmer, uneasy and obviously annoyed by Hatch's manner, wants to produce Helton immediately, so that whatever business the stranger has with him can be dispatched. But Hatch is not to be hurried. He alternately provokes and mollifies Thompson through several more rounds of seemingly idle conversation before he finally reveals that he intends to arrest Helton.

The hired man, it appears, is a fugitive from a lunatic asylum in North Dakota, to which he was committed after killing his brother in a fit of rage over the brother's having borrowed and lost one of his harmonicas. Hatch learned of his whereabouts from Helton's mother, to whom he sent a large amount of money saved over the years from the wages paid him by Thompson. Thompson is badly shaken by the story of the murder. But he so dislikes the shifty and patronizing Hatch, whose authority as well as whose motives he is inclined to question, and so resents his sudden intrusion into the peaceful and prosperous order of life on the farm, an order that has largely been achieved by Helton, that he is unwilling to let Hatch accomplish his purpose without resistance.

Giving way to his confused feelings, and the dizzying effects of the heat, he roars threats at Hatch and orders him off the farm. Helton appears suddenly from around the corner of the house, and rushes in between the other two men, confronting Hatch with his fists raised. Hatch, armed now with handcuffs in one hand and a bowie knife in the other, charges Helton. And Thompson, thinking that he sees the knife plunge into the hired man's stomach, picks up an axe and strikes Hatch on the head with it.

Helton, it turns out, is not knifed. He runs away into the woods. But Hatch is dead. After the sheriff arrives, and a posse is formed to hunt down Helton, Thompson is arrested for murder. Helton dies later in jail from injuries inflicted by his captors when he tries to fight them off.

Thompson is tried and acquitted. But the episode breaks him, and he is morbidly convinced that all his neighbors think him a murderer, despite the legal acquittal. For weeks, he wearily drags himself and his wife around the countryside, calling on people to ask them to listen to his story and to believe in his innocence.

But it is obvious that he can never come to terms with the murder. His conscience further burdened by the lie he persuaded his wife to tell, which is that she witnessed Hatch's attack on Helton and her husband's justifiable intervention, he feels at last that there is no one but God to whom he can appeal for understanding and justice. Then one night, in the agony of his sleepless thoughts, he leaps out of bed, and his wife gets up screaming in a nightmare. She collapses in a faint, and he is trying to arouse her when the boys, awakened by her screams, rush into the room. They look at him accusingly, as if they suspect he has struck their mother.

He rebukes them for their thoughts. When she has recovered from her faint, he instructs them to take care of her, and on the pretense that he is going for the doctor dresses to leave the house. Taking along a lantern and loaded shotgun and pencil and paper, he makes his way across the fields to the farthest boundary of his farm. There, sitting against a fence post, he carefully composes his suicide note. Then he takes the shoe and sock off his right foot, props the gun against the fence with the muzzle pointing at his head, and gropes for the trigger with his big toe.

The characterization of Mr. Thompson, in whose consciousness the story centers, brilliantly exemplifies Miss Porter's power of sympathetic imagination. We see Thompson from both outside and inside. And there is a good deal of conscious humor in the portrayal of the semiliterate farmer, with his absurdly pretentious name of Royal Earle, that is designed to be appreciated only by highly literate readers. But if the social and intellectual superiority of the female author to her male protagonist is everywhere evident, and essential to the total artistic effect, there is no hint of moral condescension. One who begins to read the story for the first time might expect it to reach no higher level of seriousness than that of comic pathos. But at the end Thompson is as tragic a figure as any in modern literature.

The true facts of the crucial event remain obscure to Mr. Thompson: " . . . and then something happened that Mr. Thompson tried hard afterwards to piece together in his mind, and in fact it never did come straight." Essentially, it is his own behavior that Thompson finds inexplicable. The social and moral code by which he lives, and the self-image that corresponds to the code, prove inadequate to the reality of his experience.

This disparity between the ideal and the actual is the central theme of the story, and the source of its dramatic tensions. That Mr. Thompson is provincial-minded is obvious enough. Olaf Helton is quite literally, for Thompson, a foreigner. And the reader senses that it is not, contrary to Helton's reassurance, going to be "all right" that he is "practically the first Swede [Thompson] ever laid eyes on." For, having once "laid eyes on it," Thompson exhausts his interest in Helton's foreignness, is unwilling to make the slightest effort toward that appreciation of the very real effects of different cultural backgrounds that must be achieved before it is possible for a man to meet a foreigner on the common ground of humanity. But for Mr. Thompson the coming of the foreigner, the stranger—first Helton, then Hatch—has its ultimate importance in revealing to him the stranger within himself.

To some extent, the lifelong inconsistencies in

Thompson's attitudes and patterns of behavior are typical of the provincial character—the Southern white, Protestant, yeoman farmer with baronial pretensions. A good example of Miss Porter's satiric humor at the expense of this stereotype is the conflict between Thompson's code of manly behavior, according to which "a coupla little toddies never hurt anybody," and his puritan religious convictions, on the strength of which "he voted for local option at every election." And if we see that Thompson is perhaps more than typically lazy in the exercise of his moral sense, more than commonly capable of evasive psychological maneuvers to escape self-conviction for his shortcomings as husband, father, and provider, we must also see in him, finally, an extraordinary sensitivity and strength of conscience that engages Miss Porter's and our own total sympathy, at a level of dramatic interest far above the satiric. Each of us has within him that fearful stranger whom, late or soon, he must meet and try to win over, by whatever art of persuasion, or failing that, to subdue, with whatever weapon is at hand, then to seek such justification as may be found. It would be sheerest presumption in anyone to suppose that he will acquit himself either more nobly or more sensibly than Mr. Thompson does.

The quasi-hallucinatory character of Mr. Hatch's sudden appearance on the insufferably hot afternoon is repeatedly emphasized. Thompson, with his buzzing head and dry mouth, is like a man caught in a dream. At no point does he rationally plan to rid himself of his unwelcome visitor. Instead he merely wishes him away. Hatch's role of the *Doppelgänger*, the sinister "familiar," is most explicitly suggested when Thompson feels that he has seen the man somewhere before. They have been talking about where their families come from, and Thompson is irritated by the suggestion that his grandfather might have been an immigrant from Ireland.

The stranger opened his mouth and began to shout with merriment, *and he shook hands with himself as if he hadn't met himself for a long time.* [Italics mine.] "Well, what I always says is, a feller's got to come from *somewhere*, ain't he?"

While they were talking, Mr. Thompson kept glancing at the face near him. He certainly did remind Mr. Thompson of somebody, or maybe he really had seen the man himself somewhere. He couldn't just place the features. Mr. Thompson finally decided it was just that all rabbit-teethed men looked alike.

But Thompson's lame explanation will not satisfy, of course. We realize that the person Hatch reminds him of is himself. It is Thompson who hasn't, indeed, "met himself" for so long that he cannot be sure of his identity. Cannot be sure of it, perhaps, because he cannot *tolerate* the recognition.

All the things about Hatch that are most offensive to the farmer are a mockery, a wicked caricature, of Thompson's own prejudices and pretensions. Among the characteristics of Thompson that Miss Porter strongly emphasizes in the first scene of the story, so as to fix it in the reader's mind, is his exaggerated. and calculating good humor. "When Mr. Thompson expected to drive a bargain he always grew very hearty and jovial." Determined to hire Helton at the very lowest possible wages, "he began to laugh and shout his way through the deal." It is precisely the same technique, disguising the sinister purpose of his visit, that Hatch uses on Thompson himself nine years later.

And so it is with all the subjects of their conversation—with pride of family and reputation; with
regional and racial character and prejudice; with the
trivia of male vanity, like a discriminating and expensive taste in chewing tobaccos; with every fatuity
that vitiates generous moral impulses and degrades
human relationships. Hatch holds a magnifying mirror
up to all Thompson's own destructive follies. At every
turn, he out-Thompsons Thompson. And Thompson
finally cannot bear it.

Thompson is made uncomfortable by Hatch's
coldly self-righteous contempt for the "Scandahoo-
vian" Helton, the hapless "loony," a man in hiding so
foolish as to send his mother money—an act of
affectionate concern ruthlessly exploited by the man-
hunter. Never quite consciously, Thompson sees in
Hatch's attitude a maddening reflection of his own
hypocrisy. He has enjoyed the fruits of Helton's
labor all these years, but secretly he has despised the
man, despised as "meeching" and unmanly the very
frugality of the hireling that is the basis of the
family's new-found prosperity. From time to time he
has thrown a sop to his unacknowledged bad conscience with a small increase of wages. Under the
disguise of a philosophy of tolerance for eccentricity,
he has steadfastly resisted all his wife's urgings that
he get to know Helton; "letting him alone" was
actually his way of refusing Helton human companionship.

Psychologically, it is himself, then, this intolerable
image of himself, that Thompson strikes at when he
takes the axe to Hatch. He sees Helton knifed because
he wants it to be so, wants to be rid of this living
human evidence of his own mean-spiritedness. And he
desires, and achieves, his own destruction.

He does not, of course, at this point, consciously desire anyone's death—not Helton's, not even Hatch's, certainly not his own. Even later, he consciously wants to destroy not himself, but what he earnestly believes to be a false image of himself—thereby to establish the true image as he conceives it. But, as Nance has pointed out, Thompson's "tragic flaw" is his social pride.[10] In his desperate need for justification, he can think of nowhere to turn except to the community of his neighbors.

What Thompson seeks from his neighbors, before the actual suicide follows upon the symbolic, is justification for his very existence. The legal acquittal is unsatisfactory to his conscience because it is based on lies and suppressions. His wife was instructed to testify falsely that she witnessed the slaying of Hatch. And, on the advice of his lawyer, Thompson does not reveal that Hatch told him Helton was a lunatic. His subsequent appeal to the superior court, so to speak, of his neighbors, defeats its own purpose by continuing the falsehood—as if, in his desperation, he hopes that if he only tells the lie often enough it will become the truth. But in a sense he cannot help himself. For if, indeed, he is lying about why he killed Hatch, then his whole life is a "lie"—i.e., there is nothing in it that conforms to his image of himself.

But his neighbors—all of whom, of course, are preoccupied with their own lies and confusions—cannot help him. Either they will not tell him what they really think, or they prefer to think nothing. The self-tortured Thompson is an embarrassing nuisance to them. And his wife is worse than useless to him in his trouble. He keeps hoping that one day she will tell him, in private, that she really did witness the killing, and that what she saw was just what he said happened.

But although her sense of wifely duty permits or compels her to lie in public, she will not grant him the comfort of private complicity.

Mrs. Thompson's own motives, from the brief glimpses into her thoughts that Miss Porter allows us, are not entirely clear. We might see her as acting out of an unimpeachable righteousness, one that puts direct adherence to truth above personal loyalty. But it may be that that loyalty has been seriously compromised. After the killing she deeply resents her husband. Perhaps she faults him less for demanding that she perjure herself than for having deprived her of the comfort and order that Helton brought into the life of the family. On the last, again insufferably hot, afternoon of her husband's life, when they have come back from the weary round of calls on neighbors, she stands for a few minutes in front of the refrigerator—one of the previously undreamed-of luxuries that Helton's labor purchased—feeling "the sweet coldness flow out of it." Pausing there, she loses herself in a flood of reminiscences about the hired man and his music that suggests the mood of a woman grieving for her lost lover.

But, whatever the truth of Mrs. Thompson's mind, in the end her husband resigns his appeal to her witness:

"Before Almighty God, the great judge of all before who I am about to appear, I do hereby solemnly swear that I did not take the life of Mr. Homer T. Hatch on purpose. It was done in defense of Mr. Helton. I did not aim to hit him with the ax but only to keep him off Mr. Helton. He aimed a blow at Mr. Helton who was not looking for it. It was my belief at the time that Mr. Hatch would of taken the life of Mr. Helton if I did not interfere. I have told all this to the judge and the jury and they let me off but nobody believes it. This is the only way I can prove I am not a cold blooded murderer like everybody seems to think. If I had been in Mr. Helton's place he would of done the same for me. I still think I done the only thing there was to do. My wife—"

Mr. Thompson stopped here to think a while. He wet the pencil point with the tip of his tongue and marked out the last two words. He sat a while blacking out the words until he had made a neat oblong patch where they had been, and started again:

"It was Mr. Homer T. Hatch who came to do wrong to a harmless man. He caused all this trouble and he deserved to die but I am sorry it was me who had to kill him."

Nance makes much of the blacking-out of the two words as a sign of Thompson's rejection of his wife. The black oblong patch, according to Nance, is the design of a coffin, to which Thompson has consigned his wife.[11] But I would suggest that his second thoughts might also be taken to signify a final and terrible honesty on Thompson's part, his acceptance of the fact that this last and dearest hope of human understanding has been irrevocably denied him, and that he must appear before God utterly alone.

The act of leaving a note indicates that Thompson still hopes to be justified, if not before his neighbors or even his wife, then somehow before humanity at large. His fatal pride, the hope of restoring his good name, is active almost to the end.

But not quite to the end. The instrument of his final and all-consuming purpose is the shotgun. In the last paragraph of the story Miss Porter concentrates exclusive attention upon the struggle of the man's will with recalcitrant physical reality—with the gun, with his own clumsy body. Mr. Thompson's satisfaction in hitting upon the idea of using his toe to trip the trigger—"That way he could work it"— is entirely practical. That way he could work what? His salvation, his justification before men? At that moment, no. There is no thought then of sin and redemption; no one else is there, only he and the gun. Armed cap-a-pie in his exclusive purpose, what he can do with his toe is precisely and only to blow his head off.

~~~~~~

Fools of All Nations: Ship of Fools *and Its* Background

Few serious critics have wholeheartedly admired *Ship of Fools*. The astonishing early popularity of the book—a popularity probably generated not so much by what Miss Porter had written as by the promotional activity of her publishers—was supported at first by enthusiastic reviews. But adverse comments, ranging in tone from pained disappointment to energetic hostility, began very soon to appear in intellectually prestigious journals. Aside from the chronic disposition of the savant to look with suspicion on all best sellers, there were two principal reasons for the unsympathetic response.

High-pressure systems dominated the intellectual weather in the early 1960s. It was a bad time for the appearance of *Ship of Fools*, with its rather old-fashioned, tough-minded pessimism that was bound to, and did, give offense to gnostics of all persuasions and temperaments—from the outraged Theodore Solotaroff, spokesman for what M. M. Liberman calls the "post-Freudian, post-Marxist, humanitarian social consciousness" of *Commentary*, at one extreme, to the gentle Catholic liberal, William Nance, at the other.[1]

Those who were not aggrieved but disappointed were long-confirmed admirers of Miss Porter's earlier fiction—people who were, or should have been, quite prepared to accept again the general grimness of moral outlook that has characterized her work from the very beginning. Their complaint against *Ship of Fools* was basically aesthetic. They had learned to appreciate Miss Porter's stories above all for their formal perfection. But *Ship of Fools* seemed formless. The publishers, and Katherine Anne Porter herself, called it a novel. But because it lacked, in Wayne C. Booth's phrase, "a grand causal, temporal sequence," a general "coherence of action," it seemed not to fit any very rigorous definition of the novel as a literary form. Mr. Booth confessed his own "bias for finely-constructed, concentrated plots," wherein lies "the strength of those classics, *Pale Horse, Pale Rider* and *Noon Wine*." "*There* is *my* Katherine Anne Porter," he protested—and such structuring, he implies, is as characteristic of true novels as of "classic" works in the shorter forms.[2]

Liberman's perceptive study of *Ship of Fools* and its critical reception, in *Katherine Anne Porter's Fiction*, has done much to clear the ground for my own and all future discussions of Miss Porter's "novel." As Liberman suggests, Miss Porter might have saved everyone a great deal of trouble if she had not called the book a novel in the first place. She did call it that, I imagine, just for want of a better term. But, while a Solotaroff or a Nance is not likely to yield ground on his moral-philosophical convictions, whatever the label, a formalist critic as generous as Mr. Booth might be persuaded to re-examine his definitions. (At the end of his hedging, apologetic review, Booth addressed an appeal to other readers of *Ship of Fools*: "I hope . . . that you'll find me completely mistaken in asking for a more rigorous or an inappropriate economy, and that . . . you'll explain to me how to read it better on my next try.")[3] The demand that all works of fiction have "finely-constructed, concentrated plots," as Liberman points out, is just what Booth himself called it, a bias. On the basis of that requirement, a good many books that have been called novels, not to speak of countless works of great beauty and wisdom in other genres, would be disqualified for admiration.

Further, Booth implicitly acknowledged, although he was not quite willing to abandon it, the folly of his constancy to "*his* Katherine Anne Porter" in face of the overwhelming evidence that Katherine Anne Porter's Katherine Anne Porter was now somebody else. It is a commonplace but deplorable habit of critics to deny their favorite writers the right to change. *Ship of Fools* simply is not, obviously was not intended to be, and is in no way obliged to be, anything answerable to Mr. Booth's definition of a novel. Neither is it, in its total form, like the two earlier stories of Miss Porter's that Booth mentions, or most of the other stories in her first three volumes. But this, too, is not necessarily to say that it has *no* form of its own.

Despite their great variety in length, tone, theme, subject matter, attitude, and narrative technique— comedies and tragedies, everything from very short stories to short novels—the works on which Miss Porter built her reputation, and with which critics like Booth associated her, are what I would call realistic romances, more or less tightly plotted, in which attention is centered upon the fate of a single personage. With *Ship of Fools* she moved on to something quite different, and left Mr. Booth and most of her other old admirers behind.

Actually, many characteristics of the long-awaited "novel"—what I would attempt not to define, but only cautiously to describe, as a tragic satire, basically allegorical in structure, in which many different stories of realistic romance are deliberately aborted, in keeping with the satiric purpose—are anticipated in Miss Porter's earlier work. The satiric bent is apparent everywhere, and clearly dominant in several stories. At the two extremes of cruel pathos and cutting farce, "Magic" and "The Martyr" (the latter about a fat Mexican artist who literally eats himself to death when his mistress-model leaves him for a more prosperous rival) are both satiric and allegorical. But these short pieces can easily be written off as slight and eccentric exercises. Only two among Miss Porter's longer, and obviously serious, earlier works are now recognizable as definite foreshadowings of *Ship of Fools*.

Of these two, "The Leaning Tower"—which was the first fruit of her experience in Berlin in 1931, and the title story of her third collected volume—is confused in its formal intention. It is not nearly so crude a failure as some of its more simple-minded critics have made it out to be; but the story falls between the stools of satire and romance.

The American art student Charles Upton, a kind of inferior, male Miranda, is finally of too tender a moral sensibility to perfect the gift for caricature that his first few days in Berlin had started to nourish. When Upton helps to prevent a suicide attempt by a German medical student, a fellow tenant at his rooming house, who has been a favorite subject for caricature, he is dismayed to find that his humanitarian act only encourages the Germans in their anti-American resentment of him. But to carry off convincingly the anguished self-examination that he then undertakes, Charles needs to be a little more intelligent than Miss Porter chose to make him. The story's intricately contrived symbolism suggests an allegory of fascism that might have been a preliminary exercise for *Ship of Fools*. But an emphasis on the obscure relevance of the symbols to Charles's personal psychology, which is not very interesting in itself, prevents complete success in the execution of the allegorical design.

In "Hacienda," the somber short novel in which Miss Porter records her total disenchantment with the revolution in Mexico, the method and attitude of *Ship of Fools* are clearly anticipated. The decadent Mexican aristocrat, don Genaro, at whose pulque hacienda a group of Soviet moviemakers are shooting a film about Mexico; his wife doña Julia, who is her husband's rival for the sexual favors of an actress in the company; the unlucky Indian peon, Justino, who is arrested and imprisoned for shooting his sister in an incident reminiscent of the part he plays in the film; the arrogant and venal American businessman, Kennerly, who is the emissary of the film's financial backers in California; the gentleman of ascetic elegance, Betancourt, who represents the Mexican government; the ruined, alcoholic musician, Carlos Montaña, who composes a mocking *corrido* about poor Justino and his sister; the strange, monkeylike homosexual, Uspensky, who directs the film company—all would be perfectly at home as passengers on the *Vera*.

"The revolution of glorious memory" is accomplished; but nothing has essentially changed in Mexico. In some instances, the peons have exchanged one master for another; but on estates like don Genaro's, not even that has happened. In an atmosphere heavy with the putrescent smell from the *pulqueria*, where the maguey juice is fermented to make the "corpse-white" liquor that is the source of don Genaro's wealth, family and servants and guests act out their doomed and futile, pointless life roles, which are ultimately indistinguishable from roles in the film. The film obviously will never be finished.

In "Hacienda," Miss Porter works from within the story, in the person of an unnamed American woman who serves as narrator. But with her all but total objectivity and moral disengagement, the internal narrator here is assigned an attitude very similar to that of the omniscient author of *Ship of Fools*.

Unlike "The Leaning Tower," "Hacienda" is a complete, if clearly limited, success. But with it too, the typical admirer of Miss Porter's romances was obscurely dissatisfied, and felt tempted to write it off as a lapse or an aberration. Its peculiar "inconclusiveness," in actuality the necessary and deliberately constructed, dramatic vehicle of theme, was ascribed to a failure of artistic design. Almost thirty years before the appearance of *Ship of Fools*, the now distressingly familiar complaint was made about "Hacienda," that it seemed Miss Porter had wanted to write a novel but had succeeded only in assembling "notes" for one.

A measure of humility is always due in the exercise of critical hindsight. Since there was virtually no precedent, either in Miss Porter's own previous writing or in that of other modern authors, for the formal design of "Hacienda," it is surely not difficult to understand why everyone failed to see at the time what she was aiming for in that story. And, to a lesser extent, one can sympathize even with those who promptly expressed their disappointment with *Ship of Fools* soon after its appearance. For many critics, most if not all of Katherine Anne Porter's earlier works had been the very touchstone of taste and principle. Now, she had written a book in which she violated, or worse, completely avoided, the fundamental tenets of the school in which they had received their critical training. It is no wonder that they felt almost betrayed. ("Disappointment" is the word I have borrowed from Booth's review, but an undercurrent of stronger emotion is there.)

Now, however, one can expect few people reading *Ship of Fools* for the first time to have the same vested interests that the book seemed to threaten a decade ago. A new generation of readers has grown up who should be able to look at Katherine Anne Porter's career as a whole, without a preconceived preference for the works of any period, early or late. Fortunately, the troublesome popularity of *Ship of Fools* is also past. And one can safely attempt, at last, to interpret the book on its own terms. For, in truth, Miss Porter never wrote or altered a single line of her fiction to please a critic. If nothing else, *Noon Wine* and *Ship of Fools* have at least this much in common—that they are totally the product of Katherine Anne Porter's vision, in which she was responsible to no one but herself.

At the front of the book, Miss Porter provides the following convenient list of the characters in *Ship of Fools*:

CHARACTERS

On board the North German Lloyd S.A. *Vera*, between Veracruz, Mexico, and Bremerhaven, Germany, August 22–September 17, 1931.

German

    Ship's Captain Thiele.

    Dr. Schumann, ship's doctor.

    The purser, and a half dozen young ship's officers.

    Frau Rittersdorf, who keeps a notebook.

    Frau Otto Schmitt, recently widowed in Mexico.

    Herr Siegfried Rieber, publisher of a ladies' garment trade magazine.

Fräulein Lizzi Spöckenkieker, in the ladies' garment business; from Hanover.

Herr Professor Hutten ⎱ Former head of a German school
Frau Professor Hutten ⎰ in Mexico, and his wife; traveling with them is their white bulldog Bébé.

Herr Karl Baumgartner ⎫ Lawyer from Mexico City—
Frau Baumgartner   ⎬ hopeless drunkard; his wife
Hans Baumgartner   ⎭ Greta, and their eight-year-old son.

Herr Karl Glocken, a hunchback, who has sold out his little tobacco and newspaper stand in Mexico, and is returning to Germany.

Herr Wilibald Graf, a dying religious enthusiast who believes he has the power of healing.

Johann, his nephew and attendant.

Herr Wilhelm Freytag, "connected with" an oil company in Mexico, returning to Germany to fetch his wife and her mother.

Herr Julius Löwenthal, Jewish manufacturer and salesman of Catholic Church furnishings, returning to his home in Düsseldorf for a visit with his cousin Sarah.

Swiss

Herr Heinrich Lutz ⎫ A hotelkeeper from Mexico, return-
Frau Lutz   ⎬ ing to Switzerland after fifteen
Elsa Lutz   ⎭ years, with his wife and their daughter, eighteen years old.

Spanish

A zarzuela company, singers and dancers who call themselves gypsies, returning to Spain after being stranded in Mexico.

Women: Amparo, Lola, Concha, Pastora.

Men: Pepe, Tito, Manolo, Pancho.

Children: Ric and Rac, Lola's twins, boy and girl, six years old.

La Condesa, a déclassée noblewoman who has lived many years in Cuba; political exile being deported from Cuba to Tenerife.

Cuban
> Six Cuban medical students on their way to Montpellier.

Mexican
> The bride and groom from Guadalajara, Mexico, on a honeymoon trip to Spain.
>
> Señora Esperón y Chavez de Ortega, wife of attaché of the Mexican Legation in Paris, traveling with her newly born son and Indian nursemaid Nicolasa.
>
> Father Garza ⎱ Mexican Catholic priests on a journey to
> Father Carillo ⎰ Spain.
>
> Political agitator: Fat man in cherry-colored shirt, who sings.

Swedish
> Arne Hansen, at feud with Herr Rieber.

American
> William Denny, from Texas, a young chemical engineer going to Berlin.
>
> Mary Treadwell, a woman of forty-five, divorced, returning to Paris.
>
> David Scott ⎱ Two young painters living together, on
> Jenny Brown ⎰ their first voyage to Europe.

In Steerage
> Eight hundred and seventy-six souls: Spaniards, men, women, children, workers in the sugar fields of Cuba, being deported back to the Canaries and to various parts of Spain (wherever they came from) after the failure of the sugar market.

Cabin Mates

Frau Rittersdorf	Wilhelm Freytag
Frau Schmitt	Arne Hansen
Mrs. Treadwell	David Scott
Fräulein Spöckenkieker	(David darling)
Jenny Brown (Jenny angel)	William Denny
Elsa Lutz	Karl Glocken
Father Garza	Wilibald Graf
Father Carillo	Johann, his nephew

Herr Rieber
Herr Löwenthal
Señora Ortega
Nurse and baby
La Condesa (alone)
Bride and groom
Herr Lutz
Frau Lutz
Professor Hutten
Frau Hutten
Bébé the bulldog

Herr Baumgartner
Frau Baumgartner
Hans Baumgartner

The six Cuban students occupy two adjoining cabins.

The zarzuela company: Manolo and Concha Tito and Lola, with Ric and Rac Pepe and Amparo Pancho and Pastora

The huge cast is managed with incomparable skill and economy. Only a handful of the "eight hundred and seventy-six souls" in steerage are ever distinguishable as individuals. But almost every one of the fifty-odd inhabitants of the upper decks, including ship's officers as well as passengers, is clearly portrayed —at least in indelible caricature, if not, as with an astonishing number of them, in deeper shadings of thought and feeling.

The whole action cannot be adequately summarized. The book is a vast complex of many little stories. The omniscient author's view dominates the whole. But, within that framework, many of the characters are presented also as they see themselves and each other. In just under five hundred pages, Miss Porter enters the most private consciousness of more than twenty people—of both sexes, of several different ages and ethnic groups, of widely varying personality types—with totally convincing mastery of attitude and sensibility, of mental idiom, in every case.

Some of the individuals and their stories are treated at greater length than others, of course. And

very soon after the voyage has begun, five or six
major characters emerge, upon whose thoughts and
actions attention is to be concentrated. But none of the
personal stories, even the most suspenseful and intimately detailed of them, is of paramount interest. The
book's central design is thematic rather than narrative. All the stories, as such, are woven into, and
become simply parts of, the total pattern of thematic
statement.

The book is neatly divided into three parts, each
with a title and an appropriate epigraph: Part I,
"Embarkation"—*Quand partons-nous vers le bon-
heur?* (Baudelaire); Part II, "High Sea"—*Kein Haus,
Keine Heimat* . . . (song by Brahms); Part III, "The
Harbors"—*For here we have no continuing city* . . .
(Saint Paul). But the arrangement is a deliberate
mockery of the conventional plot structure, with
beginning, middle, and end. As the epigraphs ironically
suggest, there is no definite beginning, no dependable
ending, either in time or place. Passengers board and
depart the ship at several different ports. Veracruz,
"a pestilential jumping-off place into the sea," and
Bremerhaven, totally characterless, with the water at
the docks "full of floating harbor filth around the
familiar line of idle empty ships," are purely arbitrary
terminals for a voyage that is eternal.

At one level, *Ship of Fools* can be interpreted as
a kind of prophesy in retrospect of the triumph of
fascism in Europe. The year of the fictive voyage,
1931, was a time of severe economic and political
unrest in Latin America, when many Europeans who
had settled there were returning to their homelands.
But the tragic historical irony of the German passengers' hope for a safe arrival of the *Vera* in
Bremerhaven is all too apparent. For only two years

later, in the real world, Hitler was to become Chancellor of Germany. And there can be no doubt that if Katherine Anne Porter despised fascists in general, she saw the Nazis as the worst of the lot.

The *Vera* is a German ship, with a German crew and officers. Germans form the largest ethnic group among the cabin passengers. In the despicable racist Captain Thiele, commander of the *Vera*, Miss Porter clearly intended her readers to recognize the kind of German, in a position of authority, on whom Hitler was principally to depend for his political success. And almost all the Germans on the ship share Captain Thiele's attitudes.

But it is equally clear that Miss Porter saw that the historical source of fascism is in degenerative processes affecting the whole of modern civilization. If no other fascist regime, even the most successful and enduring of them, achieved the insane efficiency and ferocity with which the Nazis ruled, still the fascist mentality is fundamentally the same wherever one encounters it. The same basic social and psychological maladies that give rise to fascist political movements afflict the people of all faiths and nations.

When it is discovered that one of the German passengers on the *Vera*, Herr Freytag, has a Jewish wife, and he is forced to give up his place at the Captain's table, no one is prepared to make an effective protest. For most of the Germans, the episode is an occasion for a mean-spirited kind of solidarity. Until then, like all the non-German passengers, they have been preoccupied with their private griefs and resentments, suffering in isolation the discomforts and vexations of life aboard the miserably overcrowded ship. Now they welcome the opportunity to join any cause, so long as it is safely *German*, that will provide the illusion of escape from themselves. Not quite everyone, to be sure, even among the Germans, approves the ostracism of Freytag.

The ship's physician, Dr. Schumann, sees with distressing clarity the irrationality and ignobility of his compatriots' behavior. But Schumann's reaction is one of fastidious contempt for the whole affair rather than of moral outrage. And neither he nor anyone else, German or non-German—whether held back by fear or by callousness or by simple indifference—is willing and able to speak decisively. Even the hapless Freytag himself, who thought that his love for his wife was beyond question, is dismayed to find that his loyalty to her has been undermined rather than strengthened by the experience.

In this and in various other episodes of the book, Miss Porter shows her keen insight into the kind of unholy collusion of good and evil—of, in Yeats's words, "the best [who] lack all conviction" and "the worst [who] are full of passionate intensity"[4]—that permitted Hitler to firm his alliances with other fascist states for attempted world conquest and genocide, while in Germany itself, in France, in England, in America, in every country of the world, believers in the equality and freedom of man uncomfortably compromised their consciences, and alternately dithered and brooded in ineffectual anxiety. German reviewers of *Ship of Fools* deplored what they saw as Miss Porter's anti-German prejudice. But, on the evidence of the book itself, the charge can be substantiated only quantitatively. There are *more* German fools aboard the *Vera* than Swiss or Spanish or Cuban or Mexican or Swedish or American fools. But, qualitatively, Miss Porter plays no national favorites in her generally pessimistic representation of modern man and his situation.

There are no wholly admirable characters in the book. They are all fools. But it is possible to sympathize with, if not to admire, some of them more than others. And among the fully developed characters, Dr. Schumann, a German, is presented in the most sympathetic light. Herr Freytag, another German, is not without dignity; he is worth redemption, if by no means assured of it. The ruined, drug-addicted Spanish Condesa, with whom Dr. Schumann has a brief and abortive platonic affair, is perhaps the most appealing of all the characters—with her capacity for witty appreciation of any human sentiment, her belief in love despite all degradations and abuses and betrayals, her universal tolerance that co-habits with despair. But the Condesa is seen all but entirely through others' eyes. The reader is offered no clear glimpse of her private thoughts. And the other Spaniards and Spanish-Americans—the unruly group of Cuban students who make an obscurely ribald joke of their frequent visits to the Condesa's cabin, the company of Spanish zarzuela dancers from whose generally larcenous intentions the Condesa and her jewels are not exempt, the smugly pious and stupid Mexican priests—do little to uphold the honor of Hispanic culture.

The Americans are a deplorable lot. The mind of William Denny, the bumblingly prurient, arrogant, ignorant Texan, is a rank thicket of prejudice and frustrated lust. Mary Treadwell, chic and poised, still very goodlooking at forty-five, is superficially attractive.[5] She is intelligent, well-educated, mentally tolerant, and capable of at least a provisional sympathy, even for some of the most unlovable of her fellow passengers. But she is unforgivably careless. It is she, in an idle and thoughtless conversation with her cabinmate, Fräulein Spöckenkieker, who gives away Herr Freytag's confidence about his Jewish wife. By the end, Mrs. Treadwell has repulsed all the advances, amorous and otherwise, that she has invited. Her frigidity is more than sexual. Having secured a divorce from her husband, she obviously would like to make the decree valid for the rest of the human race. A terrible *ennui* rules at the center of her emotional being. Her hysterical attack on the helplessly drunken and lustful Denny, when she beats his face to a pulp with the sharp heel of her shoe, is only the most superficial, physical evidence of the mental cruelty of which she is capable. The feckless pair of young "lovers," David Scott and Jenny Brown, hate more than they love. Desperately weary of each other, they are repeatedly disloyal, at least in their thoughts, while they have neither the courage nor the sexual energy to be actively unfaithful. Although not married, they are as fatally bound together in their destructive union as the couples in "Rope" and "That Tree." Like Mrs. Treadwell, they pride themselves on their moral intelligence, and are contemptuous of the grosser prejudices exercised by their fellow passengers. But should a generous impulse emerge—as when Jenny proposes that they invite Herr Freytag to dine with them, after his expulsion from the Captain's table—it becomes only another issue in their dreary and hopelessly selfish, eternal quarrel with each other.

There is only one Jew aboard. (Herr Freytag's wife is not traveling with him.) In view of the book's obvious intention to hold the Nazi mentality up to

scorn, Miss Porter might reasonably have been expected to make the solitary Jew her most sympathetic
character. But Herr Löwenthal is nothing of the kind.
Grossly sensual, gluttonous, wallowing in self-pity
and retributive contempt for Germans and all other
goyim, blasphemously cynical about his exploitation
of Christianity in his trade in religious goods ("there's
money in it," he says), Löwenthal is, in fact, one of
the least attractive people on the ship. There is more
than the technicality of citizenship involved in the list-
ing in the dramatis personae of his name among the
German contingent of passengers. In some respects,
Löwenthal is the "stage Jew" of literary convention.
But in others he is a consummate caricature of all
that is worst in the *German* national character as
Miss Porter represents it, piecemeal, in the other
Germans aboard the *Vera*. In her characterization of
Herr Löwenthal, Miss Porter interprets the German
persecution of the Jews—rightly, I think—as, to a
great extent, an exercise in projected self-hatred.

No one, of either sex, or of any race or nation-
ality, is spared—not even the author herself. In her
prefatory note on *Ship of Fools*, Miss Porter wrote:
"I am a passenger on that ship." Actually, she is
several of the passengers. The Americans Jenny
Brown and Mary Treadwell are rather obvious self-
caricatures of Katherine Anne Porter, at different
ages. But it is an important part of the design that she
also invested herself in one of the least appealing of
the Germans on the *Vera*. As Hendrick has observed,
the absurdly pretentious diary that Frau Rittersdorf
keeps on the voyage—with its self-conscious stylizing
and ignorant pedantry, its aloof pseudo-sophistication
and anxious assertions of objectivity—is undoubtedly
a parody of the journal that Miss Porter kept during

her own first trip to Europe, and that she used as the basis for the fiction of *Ship of Fools*.[6]

What might be called Miss Porter's "denationalization" of her own fictive identity in the book is an important indication of her central thematic concern in *Ship of Fools*. At one level, as we have noted, the book is about fascism. But the great folly of fascism, the absurd objective of enforcing by political means national and racial standards for membership in the human community, is revealed in *Ship of Fools* as only one manifestation of the supreme and timeless folly of man in his compulsion to set limits of any and all kinds to his human identity, to circumscribe his human potential.

The episode in which the identity theme is most obviously dominant—and the climactic episode of the book, insofar as it involves almost the entire company of first-class passengers and ship's officers—is the *Walpurgisnacht* of the Captain's ball, in Part III. It is, rather half-heartedly, a masked ball; funny paper hats are provided for everyone, and some of the passengers attempt costumes of their own devising. The traditional purpose of such affairs, of course, is to provide opportunity for everyone to escape his own identity for an evening, surrendering himself to the common festive spirit. But it is obvious from the beginning that this gathering will not achieve that purpose.

The zarzuela troupe—a band of soulless brigands whose activity as professional entertainers serves only as a cover for the business of whoring, pimping, thievery, and extortion by which they actually make their living—have taken over the Captain's party long in advance. On their own authority, they have organized a raffle for the occasion—selling tickets to their reluctant fellow passengers by various means of threat, intimidation, blackmail, and sexual enticement. During a stop at Santa Cruz de Tenerife, they go ashore to pilfer articles for prizes from the shops in town. Predictably, the ball is a debacle. Not even the precariously achieved solidarity of the Germans survives it. Several of the men aboard secretly hope to get one of the female dancers to bed during the night. But, in public, everyone wants to dissociate himself from the troupe. The question of their racial origin is endlessly, and inconclusively, debated. Are they gypsies, as they claim to be? Or worse, as señora Esperón y Chavez de Ortega reflects with horror, Spaniards posing as gypsies? Or, as one of the Germans hopefully suggests, some species of Jews? Perhaps they are of some obscure lineage that has even been debased with Negro blood—which, according to Captain Thiele, is probably after all the same thing as to say Spanish. "Scratch a Spaniard, bleed a Moor,'" he quotes with complacent Teutonic good humor, to a circle of his compatriots at lunch one day. But at the ball, the German passengers do not sit with the Captain. And, no doubt strictly according to plan, he himself is driven away very early in the evening—so choked with inarticulate rage that he can hardly keep his balance for a final bow to the room—when the dancers mock him with malicious toasts to the success and glory of the Spanish-German fascist alliance.

After a few further, pathetic attempts by some of the Germans to organize the celebration—the wretched Herr Baumgartner, for example, leads a group of the children, in goosestep, on a singing march about the ballroom—the guests disperse to their several, private pleasures and despairs. Everywhere about the ship, in the bar, in darkened corners of the deck, in the cabins and passageways, there are fights, amorous pursuits successful and unsuccessful, attempted rapes, tearful and exhausted reconciliations of married couples, harrowing confrontations of the isolated ones with themselves.

With the notable exception of Jenny Brown, who much to "David darling's" moody displeasure does join in some of the party activities, the Americans and most of the other non-Germans hold themselves aloof from the affair. Ironically it is only after returning to her cabin late in the night, rather drunk and very alone, that the diffident Mrs. Treadwell indulges a fantasy of self-metamorphosis and paints her face as a mask.

She covered her eyelids with bluish silver paint, weighted her lashes with beads of melted black wax, powdered her face a thick clown white, and at last drew over her rather thin lips a large, deep scarlet, glistening mouth, with square corners, a shape of unsurpassed savagery and sensuality. . . . Yes, it would have done very nicely—she could have worn a mantilla and comb and gone to the party masked as one of the zarzuela company—Amparo perhaps.

Sometime later, when she has almost forgotten that she is still wearing the painted mask, she opens the door to deal with the hopelessly drunken William Denny, and is startled and badly frightened when he actually mistakes her for Amparo, whom he has been pursuing about the ship all evening. Apparently, it is quite by chance that he has stumbled up to Mrs. Treadwell's door to pound on it. But, with her painted face, she is unable to convince him that he has made a mistake. And when she pushes him as he tries to drag her into the corridor, he falls, and she takes off her sandal and beats him viciously on the head and face with the sharp heel.

Psychologically, the episode is an *un*masking of Mrs. Treadwell—to herself. She discovers in herself a capacity for violence, and for enjoyment of it, that she has never before suspected. But the final irony is that the discovery has no permanent effect upon her. By the next day, she has slipped easily back into her customary attitude of cool, rather prim aloofness. She will probably never forget the incident. But she will remember it, we realize, with no very deep emotion of any kind, whether of pleasure or of remorse, and no real sense of self-involvement. It will be recalled only with the same rather idle, mildly cynical curiosity with which she observes the follies of other people.

Among those conspicuously absent from the Captain's party is that other master of the art of aloofness—in some respects, Mrs. Treadwell's male counterpart in the story—Dr. Schumann. Schumann is essentially a kind man. His sensitivity to human suffering exceeds the requirements of his professional duty. If his acts of kindness are not always quite purely motivated, they are nevertheless genuinely effective. After a bout with his conscience over his feelings for La Condesa, he encounters the wretched Herr Glocken on deck one day looking more than usually miserable, and invites him to his office for an unscheduled consultation. Herr Glocken *is* consoled and comforted by the Doctor's attentions, and none the worse off for not knowing that Schumann has offered them as much to clear his own mind of its guilty preoccupation as to relieve his patient's distress. And where Schumann cannot sympathize, he is unfailingly tolerant. But he is also a sober and proper man, very careful of his personal and professional dignity. He suffers from heart disease, and is on that account more than normally cautious not to risk excitement and overexertion. But his solicitude for his health only reinforces a native prudence. It is hard to imagine that Schumann would ever consent to put on a funny paper hat. And on this occasion he has special reasons for avoiding the kind of festivity that he would find distastefully vulgar at any time.

For Dr. Schumann has already experienced his own private unmasking, in his "affair" with the Condesa. It is profoundly disturbing to him to discover that he is in love with the woman. He is a married man, a good Catholic, a physician who takes very seriously the ethics of his profession. And the Condesa is his patient. Yet not only does he spend more time with her than he can justify in consideration of his responsibility to his other patients but he violates his own professional judgment of her case by letting her have the drugs she craves.

At a deeper personal level, the strong attraction that he feels to her is bewildering for him. She is beautiful, perhaps, but no longer young. She is ill, physically and mentally. Schumann, by conviction and lifelong habit, is something of a puritan. The Condesa, expensively but shabbily overdressed and heavily bejeweled, occupying a cabin littered with garments and reeking of perfume, stale cigarette smoke, and ether, is not quite clean even in body— and certainly not, according to Schumann's customary way of thinking, in mind. She shamelessly tries to arouse him sexually the very first time they are alone in the cabin; she lies to him, repeatedly and without conscience, about her drug-taking. She is shocked at

nothing. A young officer surprises the demonic children, Ric and Rac, hiding in a lifeboat and engaged
in an incestuous sexual act. Terribly agitated, he encounters Dr. Schumann and the Condesa on the deck
a few minutes later, and wants to get Schumann's
advice on what should be done with the culprits. But
he is too embarrassed by the lady's presence to say
frankly what has happened. But the Condesa guesses
the truth, and is completely unruffled by it.

Dr. Schumann is not the kind of man, as Captain
Thiele is, to be impressed simply by her title of
nobility. Perhaps, without doing injury to his religious
and professional convictions, he could feel pity for the
Condesa in her situation. Her husband is dead. Her sons
are political fugitives; where they are hiding she does
not know. She is being deported, from Cuba to
Tenerife, into political exile. Presumably, she is carrying the last of her possessions with her on the ship.
And when it is reported that her most valuable piece
of jewelry, a magnificent pearl necklace, has been
snatched from her by Ric and Rac and thrown into
the sea, Dr. Schumann realizes that she is probably
very close to financial destitution. But his feeling for
her is something deeper, and stranger, than pity.

He discovers with growing dismay that he loves
her *for* her despair, for her soul's darkness—not, as he
ought, in spite of it, or in the spirit of a merciful
concern to rescue her from it. He lacks the courage
of his passion. After letting her go ashore at Santa
Cruz without having fulfilled their mutual desire, he
is overcome with self-contempt:

. . . he had refused to acknowledge the wrong he had done
La Condesa his patient, he had taken advantage of her
situation as prisoner, he had tormented her with his guilty

love and yet had refused her—and himself—any human joy in it. He had let her go in hopelessness without even the faintest promise of future help or deliverance. What a coward, what a swine, Dr. Schumann told himself. . . .

The honest self-condemnation brings its own, temporary relief. And briefly, then, he is able to convince himself that the situation can still be redeemed. He sends a note to her ashore, giving her his office address and telephone number in Germany, as well as the address of the International Red Cross in Geneva. He asks that she let him know where he can write to her in the future. "He renewed his anxious inquiries for her health, hoped for a reply to the ship before it would have sailed at four o'clock. He signed himself her assured and devoted servant." For the rest of the day he occupies his mind with devising a "plan of reparation." Determined to be "simple, sensible, practical," he dreams of converting his guilty passion into "a blameless charity which could call for no explanation, could be carried on at a distance, and his wife need never know." He will see to it that La Condesa is provided for and protected, that adequate medical care is always available to her. "She was to be watched and guarded and saved from her own suicidal romantic folly."

But the greater folly, of course, is his own, in his sentimental hopefulness. And when the assistant purser brings him the news in the afternoon that his note was delivered, and that "Madame . . . said there was no answer," he is returned to a despair from which there is now no escape. Like the woman in "Theft," who steals from herself, in the end he leaves himself nothing. He has lost the Condesa, and he cannot recover the faith in himself, and in the values

of his religion and his profession, by which he lived
before he met her.

The lifelong habits of discipline are not easily
broken. After the Captain's party, Dr. Schumann
goes wearily and coldly about the business of patch-
ing up the victims of the night's follies, ending his
rounds with the hapless Denny. But then, lying down
alone in his cabin after taking his heart medicine, he
gives way to a final mood of exhausted and bitter
misanthropy. Thinking of the passengers he has at-
tended, his patients, "he rejected them all, every one
of them, all human kinship with them, all professional
duty except the barest tokens. . . . Let them live their
dirty lives and die their dirty deaths in their own way
and their own time, so much carrion to fill graves."
Going to sleep, he crosses himself mechanically. But
"his bitter thoughts . . . rose and flowed again painfully all through him as though his blood were full of
briers."

But beyond the unanswerable question that, in
one way or another, Dr. Schumann and Mrs. Treadwell and others among the passengers put to themselves after their experiences—the question "Who am
I, when all the faiths and all the loyalties by which I
have lived have been betrayed?"—Miss Porter's book
poses another and larger question. Who, or what, is
man? The question of individual identity is meaningful
only within the context of certain assumptions about
the nature of humanity as a whole. But *Ship of Fools*
raises questions about the validity of those contextual
assumptions.

Man as we see him in this book is chiefly man
as animal. The passenger on the *Vera*, constantly,
acutely, and for the most part oppressively, is aware

not only of his own physical presence but also that of the others. On the scale of bodily beauty, there are gradations only of imperfection: from the grotesquely deformed Herr Glocken, to fat Professor Hutten and his fat wife who bear a family resemblance to their fat white bulldog, to David with his premature baldness, Mrs. Treadwell with her figure "a little on the flat side," Dr. Schumann with his *Mensur* scar. Everywhere, there are the marks of aging, of disease, of dissipation and overindulgence, of injury, of genetic defect. All alike, the bodies sweat, stink, lust, and hunger. Ineffectually, they wash and douse themselves with perfume; they clog the basin drains with their hair. Occasionally, one will fall upon another in awkward lust. But much more often, they flee one another, to an open porthole or a deserted spot on the deck, gasping for air. Now and again, even to its owner, the body becomes a strange and sinister presence. Dr. Schumann, feeling the pulse in his wrist, listens in fear to his ailing heart; Mrs. Treadwell sees in her mirror the savage, sensual face of Amparo.

Caricature is Miss Porter's dominant method in the book. She has developed to near perfection the caricaturist's essential vision of the beast in man. The Huttens as bulldogs, Lizzi Spöckenkieker as road-runner, Herr Rieber as pig, are a few of many obvious examples. But all the characters, from the least to the most sympathetic and intelligent, are fitted at one time or another with animal masks of varying subtlety.

But the caricature of *Ship of Fools* is caricature raised finally to the level of tragic myth and mystery. There are many real animals in the book as well as human beings in bestial guise. And the fates of the beasts are intimately involved with those of the humans.

In the most striking episode involving an animal, it is significant that the two worlds of the steerage and the first-class passengers, which Captain Thiele has made strenuous efforts to keep entirely separate, are brought briefly together.

"Herded" onto the boat at Havana, the "eight hundred and seventy-six souls" in steerage are an object of constant and uneasy curiosity to their fellow creatures who inhabit the cabins above. The implicit comparison of the people to animals, in Miss Porter's description of the boarding, is made brutally explicit by the ubiquitous Frau Rittersdorf, who, watching with a dozen or so other first-class passengers from the upper deck says: "we did not engage to travel on a cattle boat." Frau Rittersdorf, with the ready concurrence of Herr Baumgartner, warns of the danger of contagious disease spreading through the ship from the crowded steerage. Others say they are afraid of a murderous uprising; after all, there is an avowed political agitator aboard. These cruder fantasies aroused by fear are scorned, of course, by more intelligent observers. But even in the sanest and most compassionate thoughts of the more intelligent, there is an element of condescension which such people as David and Jenny, and Mrs. Treadwell and Dr. Schumann, use to conceal from themselves the real, basic fear that they share with the Rittersdorfs and the Thieles of their world. The fear the first-class passengers suffer is that they really are, as human beings, in no way essentially different from the wretched herd in steerage; that the miserable condition of these may be, in fact, the essential condition of man, from which they as "first-class" humans, in their desperate and precariously maintained bourgeois privacies, are separated by the merest accident of history, the institutions that give them their superior status having no guarantee of permanency. And they are confronted with the irreducible, inscrutable mystery of human existence, and of the moral order of the universe, when one of the steerage passengers, a man named Echegaray, loses his own life in saving the Huttens' bulldog, Bébé, from drowning.

No one knows, and no one can very confidently guess, what Echegaray's motives are. He was a primitive artist, a wood carver—appropriately, his carvings were of animal figures. After a fight between the political agitator and a man attending Mass whose piety he insulted, the Captain ordered everyone in steerage disarmed. Echegaray was known to have been despondent over having to give up his wood-carving knife. And Professor Hutten, for reasons that are all too clear, would like to think that his leap into the water after Bébé was a disguised suicide. But the Huttens' morally evasive reaction—a pained embarrassment that degenerates finally into weary exasperation—is only the most obviously inadequate of the various responses among the residents of the upper decks. No one, not even Dr. Schumann, can come to acceptable terms with the fact of Echegaray's absurd heroism.

The death of Echegaray is the crucial episode in the development of the book's central theme, and is elaborately and carefully anticipated in earlier actions.

As everyone on the ship knows, but no one will undertake to prove, it was Ric and Rac who threw Bébé overboard. Ric and Rac "were christened Armando and Dolores, but . . . had renamed them-

selves for the heroes of their favorite comic cartoon
in a Mexican newspaper: . . . two lawless wire-haired
terriers [who] made fools of even the cleverest human
beings in every situation, made life a raging curse for
everyone near them, got their own way invariably
with a wicked trick, and always escaped without a
blow." Dolores and Armando live "in a state of intense undeclared war with the adult world"; but, as
Miss Porter is careful to point out, they do not like
"other children, or animals, either." The incident of
Bébé's rescue recalls Dr. Schumann's encounter with
the twins on a day early in the voyage, when, catch-
ing them in the act of trying to throw a struggling
cat over the rail, he acts on instinctive impulse and
makes a running leap to save the animal.

Holding them after he has pulled them away
from the rail, and looking into the indifferent malice
of their eyes—"their blind, unwinking malignance,
their cold slyness"—the doctor sadly reflects on the
humanity of the evil children: "—not beasts, though,
but human souls. Oh, yes, human, more's the
pity. . . ." A moment later, feeling badly shaken, he
sits down to take some of the medicine he always
carries with him. Then he ponders in amazement the
fact that he has risked bringing on a heart attack
with his leap to rescue the cat: " . . . he had en-
dangered his life to save the life of a cat, a kind of
animal he disliked by temperament; he was devoted to
dogs. Given a moment for reflection, would he have
leaped so and risked the stopping of his heart to save
—even his wife?"

But the first statement of the theme comes even
earlier, in the book's opening scene in the central
square of Veracruz. "A few placid citizens of the
white-linen class," businessmen and petty industrialists,

are sitting on the terrace of the Palacio Hotel, beginning the hot day with iced drinks and watching the
square come to life, when—

The beggar who came to the terrace every morning in
time for the early traffic appeared around the corner
shambling and crawling, the stumps of his four limbs
bound in leather and twine. He had been in early life so
intricately maimed and deformed by a master of the art,
in preparation for his calling, he had little resemblance to
any human being. Dumb, half blind, he approached with
nose almost to sidewalk as if he followed the trail of a
smell, stopping now and then to rest, wagging his hideous
shock head from side to side slowly in unbearable suffering. The men at the table glanced at him as if he were a
dog too repulsive even to kick, and he waited patiently
beside each one for the sound of the small copper coins
dropped into the gaping leather bag around his neck.
When one of the men held out to him the half of a
squeezed lime, he sat back on his haunches, opened his
dreadful mouth to receive the fruit, and dropped down
again, his jaws working. He crawled then across the street
to the square, and lay down under the trees. . . .

The men watched his progress idly without expression as
they might a piece of rubbish rolling before the wind. . . .

  In the superb description of the beggar, and of
the "placid citizens" as they indifferently observe
him, a passage of prose of consummate, cold artistry
that is yet resonant with unmistakable compassion,
Miss Porter all but casually indicates the basic theme
of her book, and reveals the essentially tragic attitude
that she is to maintain with incomparable consistency
through all the momentary, infinitely varied moods of
pathetic and satiric comedy that the tales of her
sundry fools evoke. The beggar, a creature who at
first glance has "little resemblance to any human

being," is progressively degraded. In his first meta-morphosis under the eyes of the "placid citizens," he becomes a dog, "too repulsive even to kick." In the next he is something lower even than a beast, not even animate, not even, among inanimate things, an object of any conceivable value—only "a piece of rubbish rolling before the wind." In his soul, every person on the *Vera* suffers at least the first of the beggar's changes, and may well suffer the next.

We must, of course, regard the beggar as well as all the other characters of the book as creations of the artist, not of God, as *factum non genitum*. To the implicit questions raised here and throughout the book —what is it in the beggar that to Miss Porter, and to us, if not to the men on the hotel terrace, reveals that he *is* human, after all, neither a piece of rubbish nor a dog, but a man?; what grounds are there, if any, for supposing that in the ultimate order of God's creation either Schumann or Echegaray, not to speak of the wretched Huttens, is a being innately superior to the ship's cat or to Bébé?—the author of the fiction provides no answers acceptable to a philosopher or a moral theologian. For she is an artist, a maker with words, not an explainer.

For the mysterious, powerful instinct of human kinship with the beast, Dr. Schumann can devise no satisfactory explanation either in his own case, with the cat, or in Echegaray's with the dog. And Katherine Anne Porter, the artist, is even less than the doctor obliged by her professional commitment to provide explanations. *Ship of Fools* suggests, perhaps, that the only true moral imperative for man, whereby he can maintain any true faith in the holiness of his humanity, is that he keep *asking* the unanswerable questions about his creaturely status. But one must hesitate to

abstract even that much, even as a *suggestion* of dis-
cursive statement, from the work of art. Katherine
Anne Porter portrays her fools, she tells their stories;
she presents; she composes. Beyond that, what she
does in *Ship of Fools* with the mystery of human
existence that is its central theme—"the uncontrollable
mystery on the bestial floor"[7]—is all that any artist
can do, has ever done, with the irreducible complexity
of human experience. She celebrates it.

Notes

1. Katherine Anne Porter:
   A Biographical Essay

1. Katherine Anne Porter, *The Collected Essays and Occasional Writings of Katherine Anne Porter* (New York: Delacorte Press, 1970), p. 449.
2. George Hendrick, *Katherine Anne Porter* (New York: Twayne Publishers, 1965), p. 15.
3. Barbara Thompson, "The Art of Fiction XXIX—Katherine Anne Porter: An Interview," *Paris Review*, No. 29 (Winter-Spring 1963), pp. 87–114.
4. Archer Winsten, "Presenting the Portrait of an Artist," New York *Post*, 6 May 1937, p. 17.
5. Robert van Gelder, "Katherine Anne Porter at Work," in *Writers and Writing* (New York: Charles Scribner's Sons, 1946).
6. Glenway Wescott, "Katherine Anne Porter Personally," in *Images of Truth* (New York: Harper and Row, 1962), pp. 25–58.
7. Ibid.
8. Barbara Thompson, "Katherine Anne Porter: An Interview."
9. Ibid.
10. Ibid.
11. Glenway Wescott, "Katherine Anne Porter Personally."
12. Barbara Thompson, "Katherine Anne Porter: An Interview."
13. Archer Winsten, "Presenting the Portrait of an Artist."
14. Barbara Thompson, "Katherine Anne Porter: An Interview."
15. Katherine Anne Porter, *The Collected Essays and Occasional Writings*, p. 355.
16. Ibid.
17. Philip Horton, *Hart Crane: The Life of an American Poet* (New York: The Viking Press, 1957), p. 286. Miss Porter does not mention Crane's having invited her to dinner.

18. *The Letters of Hart Crane*, edited by Brom Weber (Berkeley and Los Angeles: University of California Press, 1965), p. 378.
19. George Hendrick, *Katherine Anne Porter*, pp. 126–31.
20. Katherine Anne Porter, "'Noon Wine': The Sources," in *The Collected Essays and Occasional Writings*, p. 468.
21. Katherine Anne Porter, "Three Statements About Writing," in *The Collected Essays and Occasional Writings*.
22. From a speech at La Salle College, 1961, quoted by George Hendrick, *Katherine Anne Porter*, p. 15, from the Philadelphia *Evening Bulletin*, 27 October 1961, p. 19.
23. George Hendrick, *Katherine Anne Porter*, p. 15.
24. Ibid.
25. Archer Winsten, "Presenting the Portrait of an Artist."
26. M. M. Liberman, *Katherine Anne Porter's Fiction* (Detroit: Wayne State University Press, 1971), pp. 49–50.
27. George Hendrick, *Katherine Anne Porter*, p. 17.
28. Katherine Anne Porter, "And to the Living, Joy," *McCall's*, 99 (December 1971), pp. 76–77.
29. Katherine Anne Porter, *The Collected Essays and Occasional Writings*, pp. 160–65.

2. THAT HIDEOUS INSTITUTION

1. As printed in *The Collected Stories of Katherine Anne Porter* (New York: Harcourt, Brace and World, 1965) the sequence of *The Old Order* includes: "The Source," "The Journey," "The Witness," "The Circus," "The Last Leaf," "The Fig Tree," "The Grave."
2. William L. Nance, *Katherine Anne Porter and the Art of Rejection* (Chapel Hill: The University of North Carolina Press, 1964).

3. George Hendrick, *Katherine Anne Porter* (New York: Twayne Publishers, 1965).

4. The significance of the wagon driver's not turning his head has been pointed out by M. M. Liberman in his generally perceptive analysis of the moral situation in the story, of Mrs. Whipple's character, and of Miss Porter's method of controlling her reader's responses—in *Katherine Anne Porter's Fiction* (Detroit: Wayne State University Press, 1971), pp. 87–91.

4. MAN AND WOMAN

1. George Hendrick, *Katherine Anne Porter* (New York: Twayne Publishers, 1965).

2. Brother James Wiesenfarth, "Illusion and Allusion: Reflections in 'The Cracked Looking-Glass,'" *Four Quarters*, 12 (November 1962), pp. 30–37.

3. George Hendrick, *Katherine Anne Porter*, p. 103.

4. Hendrick, pp. 105–106.

5. BY SELF POSSESSED

1. Ray B. West, Jr., "Katherine Anne Porter: Symbol and Theme in 'Flowering Judas,'" *Accent*, 7 (Spring 1947), pp. 182–87. Reprinted in West's *The Art of Modern Fiction* (New York: Rinehart and Co., 1949).

2. Younger readers may not know what stockings *with* clocks are. A "clock," on a stocking or sock, is an embroidered or woven decoration that extends upward from the ankle. The origin of the word is uncertain; but the decoration often has a shape, with a point at the upper end, resembling that of a hand on a time clock.

3. William L. Nance, *Katherine Anne Porter and the Art of Rejection* (Chapel Hill: The University of North Carolina Press, 1964).

4. George Hendrick, *Katherine Anne Porter* (New York: Twayne Publishers, 1965), p. 79.

5. William L. Nance, *Katherine Anne Porter and the Art of Rejection*, p. 42.

6. The identities of Hapsy and of the baby she is holding in the dream have been the subject of much imaginative critical debate. See, for example, George Hendrick, *Katherine Anne Porter*, p. 92; Peter Wolfe, "The Problems of Granny Weatherall," *C L A Journal*, 11, No. 2 (December 1967), pp. 142–48; and Joseph Wiesenfarth, "Internal Opposition in Porter's 'Granny Weatherall,' " *Critique*, 11, No. 2 (1969), pp. 47–55. Wolfe's argument is the most ingenious to date.

7. William L. Nance, *Katherine Anne Porter and the Art of Rejection*.

8. George Hendrick, *Katherine Anne Porter*, pp. 91–93.

9. The driver of the cart in Ellen Weatherall's hallucination is a figure very like the "lank greenish stranger" with whom Miranda takes her dream-ride at the beginning of "Pale Horse, Pale Rider." Miranda's companion, too, is someone she knows she has seen before, although she cannot immediately identify him.

10. William L. Nance, *Katherine Anne Porter and the Art of Rejection*, p. 58.

11. Ibid., p. 59.

6. Fools of All Nations

1. Theodore Solotaroff, "*Ship of Fools* and the Critics," *Commentary*, 34 (October 1962), pp. 277–86. M. M. Liberman, *Katherine Anne Porter's Fiction* (Detroit: Wayne State University Press, 1971), p. 16. William L. Nance, *Katherine Anne Porter and the Art of Rejection* (Chapel Hill: The University of North Carolina Press, 1964).

2. Wayne C. Booth, "Yes, But Are They Really

Novels," *Yale Review*, 51, No. 4 (Summer 1962), pp. 632–34.

3. Ibid.

4. William Butler Yeats, "The Second Coming."

5. "Treadwell" is one of several marvelously complex, satiric names in the book. "Tread" in the old meaning of "copulate" is an important element of its ironic significance. And it is interesting that one of Boswell's more subtle whores called herself "Mrs. Tredwell." *Boswell's London Journal: 1762–1763*, edited by Frederick A. Pottle (New York: McGraw-Hill Book Company, 1950), p. 277.

6. George Hendrick, *Katherine Anne Porter* (New York: Twayne Publishers, 1965), p. 136.

7. William Butler Yeats, "The Magi."

Bibliography

1. Works by Katherine Anne Porter

FICTION

Flowering Judas, and Other Stories (New York: Harcourt, Brace, 1930; revised edition, 1935; Modern Library, 1940). Contents of Modern Library edition, with an Introduction by Katherine Anne Porter: "María Concepción," "Magic," "Rope," "He," "Theft," "That Tree," "The Jilting of Granny Weatherall," "Flowering Judas," "The Cracked Looking-Glass," "Hacienda."

Pale Horse, Pale Rider: Three Short Novels (New York: Harcourt, Brace, 1939; The Modern Library, 1949). Contents: "Old Mortality," "Noon Wine," "Pale Horse, Pale Rider."

The Leaning Tower, and Other Stories (New York: Harcourt, Brace, 1944). Contents: "The Source," "The Witness," "The Circus," "The Old Order," "The Last Leaf," "The Grave," "The Downward Path to Wisdom," "A Day's Work," "The Leaning Tower."

Ship of Fools (Boston: Little, Brown and Co., 1962).

The Collected Stories of Katherine Anne Porter (New York: Harcourt, Brace and World, 1965). The preface by Katherine Anne Porter would suggest that this is the definitive, authorized edition of the shorter works of fiction that she wrote and published before *Ship of Fools*. The volume brings together the three previous collections: *Flowering Judas*; *Pale Horse, Pale Rider*; *The Leaning Tower*. *Flowering Judas* contains "María Concepción," "Virgin Violeta," "The Martyr," "Magic," "Rope," "He," "Theft," "That Tree," "The Jilting of Granny Weatherall," "Flowering Judas," "The Cracked Looking-Glass," "Hacienda." *Pale Horse, Pale Rider* contains "Old Mortality," "Noon Wine," "Pale Horse, Pale Rider." *The Leaning Tower* contains a sequence entitled *The Old*

148

Order (including "The Source," "The Journey," "The Witness," "The Circus," "The Last Leaf," "The Fig Tree," and "The Grave"), "The Downward Path to Wisdom," "A Day's Work," "Holiday," "The Leaning Tower."

NONFICTION

The Days Before (New York: Harcourt, Brace and Co., 1952). Essays, reviews, notes, observations.

A Christmas Story (New York: Delacorte Press, 1967). Personal reminiscence.

The Collected Essays and Occasional Writings of Katherine Anne Porter (New York: Delacorte Press, 1970). A rearrangement of the contents of *The Days Before*, with additional prose pieces and eight poems.

2. *Works about Katherine Anne Porter*

BIBLIOGRAPHY

Schwartz, Edward. "Katherine Anne Porter: A Critical Bibliography." *Bulletin of the New York Public Library*, 57 (May 1953), pp. 211–47. Guide to works by and about Katherine Anne Porter, through 1952. Introduction by Robert Penn Warren.

Waldrip, Louise and Shirley Ann Bauer. *A Bibliography of the Works of Katherine Anne Porter* [and] *A Bibliography of the Criticism of the Works of Katherine Anne Porter*. Metuchen, N. J.: Scarecrow Press, 1969.

BIOGRAPHY AND CRITICISM

Barnes, Daniel R. and Madeline T. "The Secret Sin of Granny Weatherall." *Renascence*, 21, pp. 162–65.

Booth, Wayne C. "Yes, But Are They Really Novels."
    Yale Review, 51, No. 4 (Summer 1962), pp. 632–34.

Cowser, Robert G. "Porter's 'The Jilting of Granny
    Weatherall.'" *The Explicator*, 21, No. 4 (December
    1962).

Curley, Daniel. "Treasure in 'The Grave.'" *Modern Fic-
    tion Studies*, 9, pp. 377–84.

Emmons, Winifred S. *Katherine Anne Porter: The Re-
    gional Stories*. Austin, Texas: Steck-Vaughn, 1967.

Gross, Beverly. "The Poetic Narrative: A Reading of
    'Flowering Judas.'" *Style*, 2, pp. 129–39.

Hartley, Lodwick, and Core, George, eds. *Katherine Anne
    Porter: A Critical Symposium*. Athens: University of
    Georgia Press, 1969. Reprinted criticism, with an
    Introduction.

Hendrick, George. *Katherine Anne Porter*. New York:
    Twayne Publishers, 1965.

Liberman, M. M. *Katherine Anne Porter's Fiction*. De-
    troit: Wayne State University Press, 1971.

Mooney, Harry John, Jr. *The Fiction and Criticism of
    Katherine Anne Porter*. Pittsburgh: University of
    Pittsburgh Press, 1957.

Moss, Howard. "No Safe Harbor." *The New Yorker*, 38
    (28 April 1962), pp. 165–73.

Nance, William L. *Katherine Anne Porter and the Art of
    Rejection*. Chapel Hill: University of North Carolina
    Press, 1964.

————. "Katherine Anne Porter and Mexico." *Southwest
    Review*, 55, pp. 143–53.

Ruoff, James, and Smith, Del. "Katherine Anne Porter on
    Ship of Fools." *College English*, 24 (February 1963),
    pp. 396–97. Interview with Miss Porter.

Smith, J. Oates. "Porter's *Noon Wine:* A Stifled Trag-
    edy." *Renascence*, 17, pp. 157–62.

Solotaroff, Theodore. "*Ship of Fools* and the Critics."
    Commentary, 34 (October 1962), pp. 277–86.

Thompson, Barbara. "The Art of Fiction XXIX—Katherine Anne Porter: An Interview." *Paris Review*, No. 29 (Winter-Spring 1963), pp. 87–114.

van Gelder, Robert. "Katherine Anne Porter at Work." In *Writers and Writing*. New York: Charles Scribner's Sons, 1946.

Warren, Robert Penn. "Irony with a Center: Katherine Anne Porter." In *Selected Essays*. New York: Random House, 1958.

Wescott, Glenway. "Katherine Anne Porter Personally." In *Images of Truth*. New York: Harper and Row, 1962.

West, Ray B., Jr. "Katherine Anne Porter: Symbol and Theme in 'Flowering Judas.'" *Accent*, 7 (Spring 1947), pp. 182–87. Reprinted in *The Art of Modern Fiction* (New York: Rinehart and Co., 1949).

———. "Katherine Anne Porter and 'Historic Memory.'" *Hopkins Review*, 6 (Fall 1952), pp. 16–27. Reprinted in Louis D. Rubin and Robert Jacobs, eds., *Southern Renascence* (Baltimore: The Johns Hopkins Press, 1953), pp. 278–89.

———. *Katherine Anne Porter*. Minneapolis: University of Minnesota Press, 1963.

Wiesenfarth, Brother Joseph. "Illusion and Allusion: Reflections in 'The Cracked Looking-Glass.'" *Four Quarters*, 12 (November 1962), pp. 30–37.

———. "Internal Opposition in Porter's 'Granny Weatherall.'" *Critique*, 11, No. 2 (1969), pp. 47–55.

Wolfe, Peter. "The Problems of Granny Weatherall." *C L A Journal*, 11, No. 2 (December 1967), pp. 142–48.

Youngblood, Sarah. "Structure and Imagery in Katherine Anne Porter's 'Pale Horse, Pale Rider.'" *Modern Fiction Studies*, 5 (Winter 1959), pp. 344–52.

Index

153